IMAGINE!
THOUGHT-PROVOKING POETRY

BETWEEN THE LINES

Edited By Donna Samworth

First published in Great Britain in 2021 by:

YoungWriters®
Est. 1991

Young Writers
Remus House
Coltsfoot Drive
Peterborough
PE2 9BF
Telephone: 01733 890066
Website: www.youngwriters.co.uk

All Rights Reserved
Book Design by Ashley Janson
© Copyright Contributors 2021
Softback ISBN 978-1-80015-303-5

Printed and bound in the UK by BookPrintingUK
Website: www.bookprintinguk.com
YB0461G

FOREWORD

Since 1991, here at Young Writers we have celebrated the awesome power of creative writing, especially in young adults, where it can serve as a vital method of expressing their emotions and views about the world around them. In every poem we see the effort and thought that each pupil published in this book has put into their work and by creating this anthology we hope to encourage them further with the ultimate goal of sparking a life-long love of writing.

Our latest competition for secondary school students, Imagine, challenged young writers to delve into their imaginations to conjure up alternative worlds where anything is possible. We provided a range of speculative questions to inspire them from 'what if kids ruled the world?' to 'what if everyone was equal?' or they were free to use their own ideas. The result is this creative collection of poetry that imagines endless possibilities and explores the consequences both good and bad.

We encourage young writers to express themselves and address subjects that matter to them, which sometimes means writing about sensitive or contentious topics. If you have been affected by any issues raised in this book, details on where to find help can be found at www.youngwriters.co.uk/info/other/contact-lines

CONTENTS

Independent Entries

Arash Zare (13)	1
Jemma Nand-Lal (13)	2
Zahra Gul (12)	6
Keiran Rodda (12)	9
Blessing Mittoo (12)	10
Elisha Chard (14)	13
Matilda Wiggins (14)	14
Navdeep Kaur	17
Muhammad Khalilur Rahman (11)	18
Thalia Johnson (12)	20
Rihanna Bari (12)	23
Joel Spackman (13)	24
Wiktoria Jablonska (13)	27
Jude Mulhern	28
Fatimah Bhuyian (11)	31
Jaevon Andrews-Perry (13)	32
Rose Elizabeth Jones (14)	34
Maybelle Yang (11)	36
Joshua Rowe (11)	41
Aaratreeka Das	42
Sadiqah Ahmed (13)	44
Janison Sharan Jeyaventhan (16)	46
Saisha Dandekar (12)	48
Kayla Moerman (14)	50
Aiza Qayyum	52
Tanish Kirodian	54
Sophie Hanif (11)	56
Isla Caulfield (12)	58
Bethany Milner	60
Aimée Richardson (13)	62
Tomisin Shaun Awofisayo	64
Abigail Edwards (17)	66
Alimah Dugbartey (13)	68
Summer Higgs (12)	70
Reana Lata (12)	72
Abby M (17)	74
Maegan Sharp (16)	76
Aman Saleem	78
Amirah Akter (11)	80
Maisy-Ilar Moazzenkivi (13)	82
Amy Cassidy (16)	84
Chizitere Ofurum (18)	86
Aleema Mirza Hamid (14)	88
Rhianna Adams (13)	90
Mithran Loganathan (14)	92
Abdurrahman Hussein (15)	94
Inderpreet Kaur (15)	96
Phoebe Allington (12)	98
Avneet Hayer (14)	100
Thenuya Chandrasegaran (16)	102
Abhishek Rajan (14)	104
Ralph James Gilroy (12)	106
Lucy Walton (15)	108
Harry Parsons (12)	110
Rebecca Cronin	112
Aaishah Niqheth Salahudeen (12)	114
Jannat Burgaz (13)	116
Grace Betteridge (12)	118
Ayeza Siddiqui (14)	120
Summaiyya Khatun (14)	122
Sian Baldwin (13)	124
Abby Butler (17)	126
Elif Nisa (13)	128
Sarabdeep Bhatia (14)	130
Zara Hope Jones (12)	132
Desmond Jones (11)	133
Ryan Arthur (11)	134

Erin Marie Jones (13)	135	Anestina Alexiadou	179
Ella Harrison (12)	136	Madeleine Wren Friedlein (16)	180
Maryam Hussain (16)	137	Lydia Wilkins (12)	181
Jadesola Lanlokun (12)	138	Manraj Tagar (11)	182
Jannah Hussain (14)	139	Daniel Ige (13)	183
Sarah Curticean (14)	140	Salman Hussein (13)	184
Venisha Lobo (12)	141	Timothy Robb (11)	185
Hafsa Ahmed Bhatti	142	Poppy Taylor (11)	186
Tayba Mehrban (14)	143	Calum McLennan	187
Ruchira Hariyapureddy	144	Lucy Seaman (13)	188
Tammy Oyebanji (11)	146	Rahil Shabibiul (11)	189
Timothy Kennett (11)	147	Mengtong Yin (13)	190
Emma Bronwen Lacey (13)	148	Ethan Ramful (11)	191
Amy Jane Clewes (13)	149	Manjot Kaur (14)	192
Lindomar Junio (18)	150	Christian-Michael Frimpong-Mainoo (12)	193
Beatrice M Opoku (14)	151		
Jensen Warren (11)	152	Zane Attwal (14)	194
Carmen Lucia Sánchez Diamente (13)	153	Ameille Hayoukane (12)	195
		Sam Stokes (11)	196
Amelia Turner (15)	154	Jeremiel Mbogol (11)	197
Kevin Galatanu (11)	155	Paulo Alexys Gonçalves (12)	198
Connie Harris (15)	156	Hawwaa Bint Mahmood (17)	199
Mouna-Myriam Coulibaly (12)	158	Poppy Cooper (13)	200
Kewen Wang (17)	159	Suzie Jones (11)	201
Mairghréad Hodgkinson-Bostock (11)	160	Asma Siddika	202
		Reece Roper	203
Isobelle Hartley (12)	161	Izaan Ahamed (12)	204
Helen Mohammed (18)	162	Affan Aflar (12)	205
Tiffani Eluka (13)	163	Summer Houston-Earl	206
Emily Clewes (11)	164	Chrysa Tsantikou (15)	207
Puhalovian Tharshan (11)	165	Layla Rashid (12)	208
Amna Ramzan (13)	166	Muhammad Haroon Ramzan (11)	209
Eshal Raza (12)	167		
Joel Ige (11)	168	Ramlah Ahsan (11)	210
Kishore Satheeskumar (13)	169	Amy Lee Smith (12)	211
Sumaiyah Mahmood (12)	170	Mehak Khalique (14)	212
Antonio Ursanu (15)	171	Keely Rodda (13)	213
George Randall	172	Jessica Ilott (14)	214
Ruby Casemore (12)	173	Sneha Godhaniya (14)	215
Esha Malik	174	Samanta Gerulskyte (18)	216
Ellie-Jayne Scott (12)	175	Ashley Smith (16)	217
Katie Riley (14)	176		
Mikayeel Malik (13)	177		
Amber Glease (13)	178		

THE POEMS

Stop Imagining

Imagine if you were a poor boy or girl in the war-torn country of Syria
Imagine if you couldn't spare enough change to buy the cheapest thing in the cafeteria
Imagine not knowing if you or your family will live another day
Imagine having to run for your life continuously when other children your age just laugh and play
Imagine looking at your own home and seeing nothing but debris
Imagine knowing that people on the other side of the world are all living carefree
Imagine seeing your own beloved parents fall to their death
Imagine seeing innocent civilians struggle to take their last breath
Unfortunately for many children they don't have to imagine
So, let's do something to help this and spread compassion
Just because we are privileged doesn't mean we can sit down and watch things happen...

Arash Zare (13)

Murder On The Lake

I climb into Dad's police Range Rover
With our German Shepherd in the back
Dad whispers to me the details of his new case
And I know it is one I must crack

I open up my laptop
And write their name on the screen
But Mum comes in my room with a bowl of pineapple
And asks me where I've been
I lie and say I'm working
On some homework due tomorrow
She asks what it is about
And I say, "Kilimanjaro"
She nods her approval
And leaves me be
I turn back to my screen
And insert a picture of Serenity Heffley
My best friend's sister
Who was drowned in a lake
With the only thing of remembrance
Is a mouldy chocolate cake

I wake up the next morning
And remember what I have to do
I immediately jump to my device
And note she was last seen at the queue

I know I must question my best friend of a year
The deceased's only sibling
But that would make her a total mess
And totally ruin her bling
So instead I scrape my long brown hair into a ponytail
And fire off a message to my BFF
That reads: 'How you holding up?'
She replies almost immediately with: 'My life is worse than Macbeth'
I roll my eyes and marvel at what a drama queen she is
But then I remember her sister is dead
And I know I could never bring her back
No matter what is done or said

I scroll onto Instagram
And see a post from my friend
It is her with the deceased
Their hair flying behind them in the wind
The caption reads: 'I love you, sis'
I sigh and shake my head
And know how much she would flip out if she knew what I am to do
But it could be amazing; like an Agatha Christie book I read
I sniff and see who she tagged in the picture
And I am taken to a Serenity's account
But I notice something - something big
Something it will be very difficult to surmount
In one of Serenity's selfies

There is a figure lurking in the background
But there are two things about that that are disturbing
And both leave me spellbound

It is something that makes me so twisted and angry and full of revenge
I scream in frustration and throw my phone across the room
The figure in the background holds a very long knife
And after I zoom
I see that it is the one person I dread
My best friend
One of the only people I trust completely
But I wonder what she was to intend

There is the obvious that doesn't make sense
Serenity drowned; she wasn't stabbed
But maybe the knife was just a threat
Before my friend murdered her sister and she was tabbed

I tell myself it's not true
But here I am just facing facts
But I suppose there really is only one way to find out
And hopefully the result will make me retract

I march out of my house
And only go just across the street
I bang on the door
But Mrs Heffley says she is busy cooking meat
I stay and say I need to see my friend

That it is urgent
So Mrs Heffley calls her only remaining child down
And I thank god she is not accompanied by her servant

As soon as I am sure Mrs Heffley cannot see us
I snarl at her and call her a liar
I call her some more rude names and that we are no longer friends
And finally that I know what she did to her sister

My ex-friend just laughs
Not evilly - just how she would normally
She says I must be a bit muddled and confused
Slowly she smiles warmly
She hands me a coffee and I take a sip
She tells me she is getting over her sister a bit
She says she never really liked her anyway
And finally she asks if I would like to sit
I reluctantly agree
And she goes in-depth telling me the knife was just a joke
But then I start to feel a little bit woozy
And darkness surrounds me like a puff of smoke

I wake up, my arms and legs shackled to the hard bed
It's then I realise I'm in my ex-friend - a murderer's - grasp, anything can happen
I try to scream but my mouth is taped shut
And I know there is nothing left but for me to imagine...

Jemma Nand-Lal (13)

Imagine

I magine the unimaginable,
M ysterious and magical,
A nything, including your wildest dreams,
G oing to great extremes,
I n search of a way,
N ever giving up and turning away,
E ven risking your life to save the present day.

The bitter wind flinging knives at you,
As the sky hurls snowballs at your face,
Yet trudging onwards and seeing through,
And realising you're doing this for someone who,
Is true to your heart and inspires you.

According to legend people believe,
The Well of Erased Memories is concealed,
No one yet has achieved,
This extraordinary quest and retrieved,
The treasure it holds,
The glory it can behold,
Which is simply worth more than gold.

According to legend people say,
This arduous mission triggers dismay,
However once reached the sacred well,
Bubbling with excitement you would have felt,
Your legs buckle,

And engulfed in ease,
Soon you end up on your knees.

Gazing longingly with awe,
Like never before,
You stare transfixed,
Observing the picturesque views,
That are untrue,
The vast azure waters are a sheet of glass,
And are like a mirror to the clouds that pass,
Large snowdrops nod their heads,
As they dive towards the water's edge,
While the sunset's smile broadens,
Slowly becoming a crimson,
The well's fury intensifies,
Letting out a deep and deafening cry.

It is the well's duty to guard,
The potion from people afar,
Only an honest and wise person will succeed,
And erase the wretched memories.
You must solve a riddle,
To get to the middle,
While you suffer in harsh conditions,
Next you need to chant,
Which will grant your accessibility,
Ancient songs and hymns,
Allowing you to get in.

Now able to move forward,
Not regretting the past,
But able to throw the moment away, at last,
Walking back home with light shoulders and relief,
Living life without any grief,
This time is precious,
This time is priceless,
Before you make another mistake again.

   I magine the unimaginable,
 M ysterious and magical,
  A nything, including your wildest dreams,
  G oing to great extremes,
   I n search of a way,
  N ever giving up and turning away,
  E ven risking your life to save the present day.

Would you do it?

Zahra Gul (12)

If Superpowers Were Real

I f superpowers were real, I would love to see them.
F lying would be incredibly fun. No paying for aeroplane flights.

S peed would be nice to win every race and win the Olympics.
U npredictable things happen with superpowers.
P erhaps the world would be chaos.
E xtraordinary things happen with superpowers.
R eal? Don't be silly
P eople would love to have lots of powers.
O ther people might hate having superpowers.
W ould you like to have superpowers?
E veryone likes different superpowers.
R omantic powers would be awesome.
S ome powers are extremely dangerous

W hat if the world was full of superpowers?
E veryone would be amazed
R eal powers are invisibility etc
E veryone might enjoy the world then.

R eal powers to get rid of illnesses would be nice
E veryone would be healthy and happy.
A ll superpowers are nice
L oads of people would think the world was a new place.

Keiran Rodda (12)

What If We Were All Equal?

What if we were all equal?
Would life be the same?
You commit a crime,
Who's to blame?

You bounce a ball,
It comes right back,
You feel like someone's taking your place,
Counterattack.

Someone does evil,
With a name to maintain,
A lie causes trouble,
But the truth causes more pain.

A lesson to be learnt,
A story with a moral,
We are all as guilty as the other,
An innocent person dies,
It's seen as normal.

Same thoughts,
Same opinions,
Imagine everyone jobless,
Same positions.

Imagine everyone being criminals,
Same convictions.

Imagine being the same race,
No more 'Black Lives Matter' signs popping
up into the sky,
No more black men being killed for no reason why.

This should have been the world in the first place,
Black lawyers being able to get a case,
Walking down the street being able to show your face,
Because you know that 'they' won't kill you with any little mistake,
But this is not the case.

They say the blacker the berry the sweeter the juice,
A black kid dies,
The lighter the killer,
The more of an excuse.

You take something out of your pockets,
Automatically, 'it's a gun'
Locked and loaded,
Ready to shoot,
Pow!
And that's you done

You see the struggle a normal black person goes through,
If we wear a hooded sweatshirt, we are labelled intimidating,

If you wear a chain, you're now a thug,
And once your pants sag you now sell drugs,
If a black girl wears long nails they are labelled low,
But if a white girl does, it is a 'new style in a fashion show'.

A Muslim person is spotted,
A terrorist is in sight,
Aim, shoot, fire
Another police attack is in light.

Police are supposed to protect everyone,
But isn't that a lie,
It's weird that the government say that,
When every day innocent people still die.

All these stereotypes,
Sum up lies,
There're sharp as a needle,
But believed by many people.
It's like our skin is illegal,

Once someone sees it,
It's like they've seen a ghost,
Now look at the words in bold,
Strong meanings,
Defiantly not feeble,
But would they all exist,
If we were all equal?

Blessing Mittoo (12)

Mask

Imagine a world with no planes in the sky,
No boats or flights to catch your eye.
Now imagine a life with no pops of colour,
Doesn't life seem so much duller?

Now imagine a place with no life,
No people, no streets that are rife.
Imagine the population falling,
When there isn't a time for your calling.

Think about not being able to pop to the shop.
No break, no milk, has the pin dropped?
If people won't wear a mask,
To do a simple everyday task.

Our life will be like these lines,
No colour, no life and no rhymes.
Oh how boring that would be,
Nothing to do or see.

But this is how we will be,
If people don't stop thinking, *oh it doesn't apply to me.*
So for heaven's sake wear a mask,
Don't go and do an unnecessary task.

We're all in this together,
And if not, then this will be our forever.

Elisha Chard (14)

We're Only Children, Set Us Free

The sun-speckled roof of my parents' old apartment,
Shining in the hue of golden songbird fire erupting from outside the window.
Bleary-eyed children wandering, aimless, mindless, power-hungry delinquents,
Bickering in birdsong as the wind rustles the dying remains of natural life.

The sun is hope, a foreshadow of potential prosperity,
Yet when it goes down, the sky filling with exploding stars.
Scars slicing the jade-black sky, fragments of glass, breaking the skin,
The veil is lifted, just for a moment, and we see the cracked earth in all its ruin.

The tally on my wall, my prison cell, counting the days in unprecedented fury,
We move in collective, yet divided by the thing that brings us together.
A hand guiding toward yet pulling apart with force unnatural, inhuman, alien,
Our whole world is alien, from the bath of mist, enraged with malice to the sun, green with envy.

We have been alone for fourteen weeks, time slipping in a wormhole of despair,

Fleeting seconds of bliss puncture the balloon of panic suffocating us.
Divide and conquer, a motto adopted by the children as the strong bark orders,
The weak simply mingle, zombies to the control of hunger, frailness and incapability.

Emerald eyes turn storm, life drained from the very souls of the once carefree,
Lost in the mist, a twisted shadow of a child once loved.
A fading glimmer of the youth of yesterday succumbed to today's reign,
The warmth is gone from the heart leaving only the chills to wrack the bodies.

We wanted this, we thought that this was right, the best option,
Sick of the endless tyranny of adults, of the government, of authority.
Opening new doors into the facade that was an adult-less haven,
The dystopia masked in sweet-scented freedom and carefree hope.

If only our eyes were not blinded by such evident, tempting lies,
Our childish brains overwhelming the suspicion regarding the wager we signed.
We are only children, funny how times change, moments become history, pretence becomes reality,

We're old enough now we used to cry, now we sob into tear-soaked sheets.
We're only children, set us free.

Matilda Wiggins (14)

Dear Grandpa, Imagine...

Dear Grandpa, imagine if I had a ladder so high
That allowed me to peek through the dark blue sky

I would climb that ladder without thinking twice
To see you once again, one last time

Imagine if I did meet you once
I would hug you tight until the end of time

I would tell you stories and my deepest thoughts
Like Grandpa, you used to do once

I would relive those moments as a kid forever
Because Grandpa with you I feel safer than ever

But I know, oh Grandpa, you look at me from above
Smiling brightly through that big shiny moon

You left me too early, you still had to look at me grow
But as the saying goes... 'The prettiest flowers are picked first'

You're still alive with me, in my heart and my soul
You still come in my dreams, to scare away my darkest thoughts

I still miss you deeply but I know you're in a better place,
Dear Grandpa, imagine if I could meet you once again...

Navdeep Kaur

Imagine If The Sun Collapsed

Gigantic red things in the sky,
Why dry our world till we have no tears to cry?
Why only leave some to survive
And take the rest of life?

Woken up in the morning, less will to live.
The great red sky vanished, a dark void left.
Celebrations announced, dreams scorched.
Solar flare, take me away, don't leave us all to fade.

Heat, extremes, drought, death.
Essentials to life, whisked away in a puff of steam.
100 years ago this slipped all imagination,
Preparations never made, illness clouded all minds.

Great sickening, why didn't you take me?
We're all crippled, all easy to kill.
Almost none left, why did you leave us for dead?
The burrows were made, hope returned.

Cooler air, refreshing, why did thee genius have to die?
He thought of the burrows, giving us a chance to live.
Life was better, light at the end of the tunnel.
Now look at us, like dwarves of legend.

We dug and dug, like soldiers in trenches,
Finding no nourishment from the hard toil.
Suffering to help the rest, we had hope.
How naive we were to think the suffering had ended.

The one tunnel, the one exit,
They thought it would end their suffering.
How wrong they were, dying painfully.
Would life ever have meaning again?

Generations later, advancing like cavemen,
Rediscovering what we didn't need before.
New ice-bringers were needed,
They thought I would do well.

Up to the tunnel, up out of the burrows,
Snowy winds, icy air, could you feel it at absolute zero?
So many bodies, as far as the eye could see.
You would think we walked into Death's domain.

Ice in my hands,
Numbness all over,
Why was I chosen?
It all turned black...

Finding new people, reconnecting humanity,
Surviving, adapting, as all life has had to.
It will all end by the severe cold or the scorching heat,
One heatwave, one blizzard, could end it all.

Muhammad Khalilur Rahman (11)

What Is Imagination?

Can you imagine imagination?
Would it look like a snake?
Would it always be awake?
Would it live for all time?
Would it, like me, talk in rhyme?
Would it be kind or would it be cruel?
Would it look like the old, crabby teacher from school?
Would it be one shiny, glittering mass
Or would it take the form of a beautiful lass?
Would it have the head of a donkey, or ears of an ass
Or would it be spiky and green like grass?
Would it be light and soft as a feather
Or would it be cold and feel like leather
Or would it feel like mixture of the weather?
Would it look like a huge kaleidoscope of colour
Or a sea of rainbow, just much, much fuller?
Would it be an animal or a supreme god?
Would it be stinky and smell like raw cod?
How would it sound?
Would its voice be a mixture all round?
Would its voice be loud?
Could you tell if it was proud?
Let me tell you loud and clear,
It's something you can both love and fear.
For different people it is different things,

Imagine - Between The Lines

What it is for you could be anything.
An eagle with some giant wings,
A fairy who loves her dairy,
Or something actually quite scary!
How it feels is up to you,
And whatever you decide to do.
Let it run free and wild,
And play with it just like a child.
So, tell your littlies a little story,
And then see their imagination beam in glory.
In a couple of years, what shall you find,
But the imagination of your child's mind.
Smiling patiently, as clear as day.
For imagination cannot be hidden or swept away.
So, to answer the big question there,
A dead imagination is quite rare.
Imagination is all inside your head,
But it's much more worthy when it is fed.
And more worthy than any gold and jewels,
Although it is wasted on a lot of fools.
Imagine life without it.
It would probably give me a fit.
What would be the point in life?
It would fill my heart with dread and strife.
So now that it's time for me to say 'goodbye'
I'm 100% honest I didn't lie.

Imagination is really good for you,
Especially when it gets you out from your blue.

Thalia Johnson (12)

Galaxion

Imagine if there was a galaxy full of friendly aliens waiting to see you arrive?
There would be an eternity of pets to lick you in the face:
Beware if you are allergic to such cute faces and unfamiliar bodies
Make sure you come in a suit!

Imagine if there was a world full of satisfaction?
Beware, you might be a little bit jealous (of those in space)
Of this unique society!

What if you were immune from getting burnt by this oven-like sun?
The sun which is actually made from billions of stars that look friendly
But they are actually not
This is a caution for your vacation!

Imagine if you could jump across all of those orbs moving in an elliptical orbit around a massive star?
But do not jump on Mercury unless you want it to take you as its dinner
I am very sure that you would not want that but just your own dinner!

Rihanna Bari (12)

Imagine Being Me, A Soldier

Imagine being me, a soldier,
A soldier who fought the bloodiest battle,
The battle to get home,
The battle about me,
The battle to save our country,
The battle to save the world,
The battle to become a hero.

Imagine being me, a soldier,
Bang, zip, thwack - running, dodging,
Soldiers falling everywhere.
Leaping, firing, a burst of bullets, then moving forwards a bit,
Slow progress but good progress,
Bang, clank, the guy next to me is dead,
Blood oozing out of his head.

Imagine being me, a soldier,
Just imagine me four hours earlier,
Sleeping on an uncomfortable bed,
The nerves knowing that later, most of your fellow soldiers,
Won't go home to see family.
Won't ever see the light of day again,
The distraught look in their eyes.

Imagine being me, a soldier,
Life on the line, this place is hell,
World let me be spared just for a moment,
Just give me the power to push on.
The sea turning red, blood fills the water,
Splash! I step in a pool of blood,
The treacherous land, sand dune after sand dune,

Imagine being me, a soldier,
Help me world,
Life must go on.
We must save the people around us, to never die in vain,
Just help me world, help our fallen,
Help us, the people of Europe,
The people of the world.

Imagine being me, a soldier,
Leaping barricades,
Shooting anything that moves,
Nearly there - 400 meters,
I can do it,
Just save me,
I feel adrenaline rushing.

Imagine being me, a soldier,
Shell fires - bang,
I dive for cover like a football goalie, diving for the ball.
Oh, how I would love to watch a match again, to support my local team,

Memories flood my mind,
For a split second I notice the enemy.
Finger poised over the trigger, can I do it? Can I shoot the man?

Imagine being me, a soldier,
Bang, bang, bang - I fire a burst of bullets,
He falls in a heap, eyes immediately blank,
I know I have just ruined someone's life.
The family in tears as they receive the note,
Oh, what an awful man I am,
I'm glad they don't know it was me,
I'm glad they don't know it was me.

Joel Spackman (13)

If Only

The world is dying
Children are crying
There are animals going extinct
We could have changed this
But now we're in danger
And our only boat is sinking
If only we stopped this by looking around
Seeing the damage that we have done
Scared of monsters but that's what we are
There is no future if we carry on
If only we woke up with one thing to do
Save our planet and do what's good
Maybe the brightness would shine through
Although all the people are still very rude
No matter the colour of anyone's skin
We should still all be treated the same
No matter the size or beauty within
We're all humans that are slowly dying
If only we woke up with one thing to do
Save our planet and civilization
However 'if only' are just two words
That can't go against our cruel world
'Cause no one can save it except ourselves
But how can we do that alone?
We can't.

Wiktoria Jablonska (13)

The End - A Message For Us

Muffled voices through the door,
Cold stone of the kitchen floor,
Everyone in there but me,
Is there something I ought to see?

They say the world's going to end,
I don't know how, or why, or when,
Everyone knows except me,
I don't want to know, I want to be free.

Children are screaming in fear,
Why are they crying right here?
Everyone's sobbing but me,
I'm just the girl who doesn't want to be.

They turn the telly up loud,
The man reports of a deadly sound,
Everyone's watching but me,
I'm the one person to disagree.

The rumbling starts to begin,
I go to my bed and tuck myself in,
Everyone's gone outside,
The laws of nature they don't want to abide.

The day has come for the end,
Everyone has a last message to send,
Everybody but me,
This 'tragic' even is setting me free.

Bright light approaches,
Booming loud sound,
Crumbling walls fall,
Tumbling down, down,
Scream and cry,
Abut to die,
Pray to God,
For your life,
The end is here.

They tell me to come in close,
A final even to say adios,
Everyone's sad but me,
We're all just things like the sea.

I look around and realise,
Why we should all be terrified,
I am going to die,
No more living, just goodbye.

I shut my eyes and breathe,
Trying so hard to believe,
Holding my family tight,
A solitary tear rolls below my eye.

I don't know how or why or when,
Because I didn't pay attention,
But long ago my world did end,
And now I am part of history.

The era who killed the world,
And the last one at that,
I wish I could go back in time,
And tell every one of you
To stop!

Jude Mulhern

My Paradise

In everyone's mind,
There's something different to find.
Some think about being immortal.
Some think about their life portal
But not everyone has the same mind.

I think about a life ruled my kids.
Though all young people might dream of staying kids,
But I'm able to live my dreams.

When things don't go my way,
I closed my eyes and they open up into paradise play.

Everyone is free there,
Over there my dreams come true out of thin air.
They can do whatever they want,
Whenever they want.

In my kind of paradise that makes me drool,
They know nothing about school.
Homework to them isn't even a real thing.
The only thing you learn is how to be a kid with wings.

For us our entertainment is playing games, being with your friend and being free.

Sadly, I still come back to the real world,
But being in the world gives me a break from life that's curled.

Fatimah Bhuyian (11)

Black Lives Matter

You see us black beings are just like any other human being.
We have a mind of our own.
We are smart.
We are strong.
We come in different complexions and we all have our own reflections.

People think we're monsters or animals,
they call us names and discriminate and police love to pull the trigger on us black folks!

"BLACK LIVES MATTER!" we shall scream.
Remember what Martin Luther King said... "I Have A DREAM..."
We should put down our guns and throw away our knives!
'Cause if people are gonna discriminate us
we should show them they aren't right.

Black or mixed-race, it doesn't matter.
We shouldn't have to go through pain or depression for what colour we are.
George Floyd was an innocent man who didn't cause no harm, and police stood on his neck as if he was a piece of trash.
"I CAN'T BREATHE!" he said but they didn't care.
They took his life, oh what despair.

Jerome Rogers was only twelve years old, police shot him for having a toy gun.
He was black as well you see.
I am not racist myself, but these policemen are a bunch of enemies to you and me.

BLACK LIVES MATTER YOU SEE!
I'm scared I'll die but not by the police, but from being stabbed 'cause that's how it goes on the streets.
I'm from the UK and I have seen things.
Seen not on the news but on social media or YouTube!

If 'Black Lives Matter' why are you killing and stabbing other black people?
Let's say it was a family member, you would be shocked or outraged wouldn't you?

DROP the knives and guns!
Stop The Violence!

RIP Mark Duggan, Jerome Rogers, George Floyd and don't forget RIP to all my brothers and sisters.

Black Lives Matter.

So do Me and You!

Jaevon Andrews-Perry (13)

Imagination Mountain

Imagine a mountain that looks unwelcoming.
Narrow paths up the side are uncertain and always changing.
Rocks suddenly fall - it is an anxious time.
Clouds loom over, no flowers or sunshine.

Imagine a mountain with nettles growing in rifts,
Unstable trees that cling to the treacherous cliffs.
Sharp paths are dangerous and ever so steep,
All daunting, with rivers near, perilously deep.

Imagine a mountain that causes destruction all the time,
That creates an alarming, hazardous climb,
Rocks that surround are exposed and never forgotten,
The boulders around mean deadly falls are common,

Imagine a mountain that creates jeopardy night and day,
The malicious mud that swallows people who stray.
The creatures are future changing and can decide your life,
The inclining steep adds to the dangerous strife.

But...

Imagine a mountain, when climbing down there is joy,
On the other side there is nothing to destroy,
Flowers, trees and nature greet you as you travel to the ground,
As earth returns to usual, happiness is found.

Imagine the decline - amazing wonders tranfix effortlessly,
It is a powerful, thrilling and a blissful place to be,
Imagine a place to be admired for its motivating views,
A place for adventure, you can take any wonder path you choose.

Imagine a mountain that has its ups and downs,
It can have its challenges, but smiles are seen instead of frowns
It's a once in a lifetime experience which can improve our perspective,
It can change the way we look at life which can be very effective.

Imagine a place where all hope can be found,
A mysterious place, where vital lessons are abound.
Where the rainbow blows the storm away,
This place is where happy events can happen every day.

Now... imagine lockdown is a mountain.

Rose Elizabeth Jones (14)

A Glimpse Of Our World

If we could
Take a moment
And just
Imagine the world
Like it was

White clouds
Across the sky
Deep blue oceans
Calm and still
Green fields full
Of spring buds
Lush flowers unfurling
In the sunlight
Animals
Seeing the new
Meeting the old
Happy cries
Of mothers
Hearing their children
Take their first cries
Colours splash
Across the sky
Cold rain
But warm sun
Butterflies trace

The path of spring
Over and over
Alight on a flower
Wings fluttering
Then flying
Flying
Flying
Into the sky

Sun beating down
Warm light
Shining through
The thick clouds rolling
Across the sky
Curl your toes
In the hot sand
Shiver and squeal at
The waves
Crashing
Crashing
Onto the shore
Rolling over
And over
Splashing
In the cool waves
And ocean spray
Warm light of summer
Beating down

Pick up the
Smooth pebbles
And shells
Of another world
Cool and creamy
Against your warm skin
Run around
Around
Laughing and kicking
Up the sand

Trees
Decorated
In crimson
And gold
Up and down
The street
Leaves
Floating
Fluttering
Down to the ground
Smell of fresh
Hay and light
Breeze goes flying
Down the road
Through the open
Windows and doors
Warm colours of

Autumn flood my vision
Wet leaves
Drenched in rain
And hope
Carpet the road
Like a walkway
Of fire

First slowly
Then quicker
Until it's everywhere
Blinding my vision
Snow
Ice
Drops of frost
Cling to the grass
Like jewels
Glittering
Everything is a
Pure white
That my eyes
Find mesmerising
Attracted to
The winter glow
The hard ground
Blanketed
In white
Snowflakes

Like feathers
From the sky
A gift
From the heavens
To the Earth

Our Earth
Our world
Our choice.

Maybelle Yang (11)

If I Were...

If I were a superhero flying through the sky,
The first thing I would do would be to fight a bad guy,
If I were a chicken in a big red barn,
I would most definitely try to take over the farm,
If I were a Weetabix trapped in a box,
I might try to break out of the package where I was locked,
If I were spider spinning all my webs,
The one thing I would want to know is where I'd go next,
If I were a businessman doing all my paper,
The main things I would need would be a pencil and a stapler,
If I were penguin swimming in the sea,
I would race the others until I was in the lead,
Another thing I would love to be,
Is hundreds and thousands as small as a flea,
I would never get eaten or crunched in teeth,
Instead I would go and live in the sea,
Happy as a clam and free as a bee,
But the one main thing I want to be
Is just to be normal and normal is me.

Joshua Rowe (11)

His Refuge

Russet eyes, mellow and swift
Twin pools of ceaseless warmth
Pride, euphoria churning glee in its depths
As they dart swiftly, restless
They wrinkle, ever the tiniest bit
From the pull of a smile
Feeling glistening pearls from the embrace
Of imposing flesh, his lips
Tainted blasphemous red, fading into mellow cherry
Cheeks dusted with crimson flush, that whispers
Sweetly, tales untold
He steps, heels purging hollows in creaking wood
Towering, head swimming in mist
Lights glisten and dim in deadly melody
Hues of scarlet and amber, flooding tenaciously
His olive skin dappled in spurned gold
Resonating an unheard chorus, singing its lamented woes
His drapes taint as they follow, his unseen trail
Flittering and cowering, under the roaring tamed
The first note, tentative
His voice rumbles, an earthly jingle
Gushing in his chest,
His luscious tresses, slipping past unbound shoulders
Virgin of synthetic odours, their imposing burning smell
Blossoms of the humid summer breeze,

Of forgotten youth and suppressed desires
Freed, wilting
Moisture clings to his flesh, puttering as he summons upon a grand finish
To an ending saga
Unfolding brazen dreams
Crazed he awakes, to filament lights and grey suits
Longing for a dream unseen,
The familiar heels and mellow notes
Clashing vehemently against broiling drums
Afraid he seeks refuge in burning cologne
And roughened stubbles
He wishes he had the courage, to clad himself
In his views, in his gaze,
Perhaps one day, he smiles wistfully
He shall be indifferent, shall be brave, shall indulge
In his 'unnatural' preferences.

Aaratreeka Das

The Wish Of Death

There Death lays,
On a bed of dandelions.
His bony hands pluck one from the field he stays,
And he closes his eyes.

He recalls the chatter of children,
The pleads with the doctors.
"Please don't let her die,"
I'm sorry. He is sorry. He is always sorry.

What is he? If not a creature so cruel.
These lives are nothing but a task on his list.
What's next? Enter a school?
I don't want to do this anymore. He never did.

The image of a blissful family replace the phosphenes in his eyes,
Cries of celebration, of a happily ever after.
But only because he is not there, he no longer hears their cries.
"I wish everyone lived forever"
So do I. He does. He really does.

Smiles shared all around, hugs tighter than a knot,
The last thing left to do is to sign to be discharged.
Pack up the night bag and wig then head to the car lot,
"Mum did it, the doctors were wrong, she made it out."
I'm happy. He is. He wouldn't be anything else.

If only everyone lived forever.
No pain, no grief, no graves.
Just life, one and all together.
Just life.

And then, he decides.

Death opens his eyes.
He takes in the birds soaring above.
Just life.
The clouds spotting the sky.
No death.
The near-ripe apples hanging down.
Just life.
How the leaves have been painted green again.
No death.

He smiles and closes his eyes
Bringing the lonely dandelion to his lips.
And he blows.
Just life, no death.

And the petals join the wind, right before Death fades along with it.
Alas, the only wish of Death.

Sadiqah Ahmed (13)

Imagine

They want me to pick my pen and start to imagine,
Of journeys underwater or inside lost caverns,
Yet, really my mind starts to bewilder,
For there's more to imagine than a real-life thriller.

I imagine of a world where love is without bounds,
Without the requirement of certain backgrounds,
Of black, of white, of yellow, of brown,
Does it really matter who's wearing what gown?
For men and women have freedom of choice,
To express themselves and raise their voice,
Yet, something's always preventing their shine,
So equality and love is on the decline.

I imagine of a world of sunny skies,
Where we don't hate or terrorise,
A world of hope, of aspirations, of dreams,
Where we don't tear each other at the seams.
Yet, this is all in my imagination,
Made from my thoughts, my words, my fascination.

Yet, why do I have to imagine such a world?
Why can't I spend hours dreaming of an underworld?
Because this world is a world of despair, of darkness, of pain,
A world where even the coherent goes insane,
Although, credit is given to those of merit,

Of pure heart, of courage, of strong spirit,
But if you want me to imagine, what I picture
Is a world where all of us is a victor.

Yet, can we make this a reality?
Working together to make this a global decree,
Imagine, imagine, they told me to dream,
Of a world to escape to, a world to beseem.

My world isn't one of unicorns and fairies,
It's a world of love and universal sanctuaries,
It's a world of one I wish to create,
But for now I'll leave it for my imagination to narrate.

Janison Sharan Jeyaventhan (16)

The Code

I was told to stay quiet, to not speak or to slip it out,
But I just could not help, the words that flooded out of my mouth.
I went up to my boss and told him what I had done wrong,
But he just would not have it and kept going on and on
"Why did you do what you have done?
Our future was in your hands and you have ruined it by one!
What shall I do to punish you for your sin?
I know what to do... and I'm sure you'll never win!"

He held me captive, till my punishment was made
As he walked up to the chamber, I dreaded that punishment that forbade
"You have been in this chamber for far too long,
Time to see where your fate will belong!"

"Please my boss, have mercy on me,
I know I was wrong, just please set me free"

"Never," he said, "till you've paid for your crimes!"
And there went the screen up in a chime
"Your punishment for sinning against
You'll never ascend to Heaven or Hell!"

260 years old
And there goes the legend
As it was foretold

And there I stood
As age passed me by
Not a wrinkle on my skin
Not a white hair on my chin

Inside my heart is dying
But I still manage to fake a smile
Trying to keep myself from crippling away
I will never die at the end of the day

And the moral of the story,
Well, I guess we will never know
Except for the one thing
Never reveal the code!

Saisha Dandekar (12)

Eclipse

Moonlight
Weary, unappreciated, dull,
But silvery nonetheless.
It warps and distorts,
Yet it makes the sun
so much clearer.
To be there but not be seen
Known but unloved.
Forever cold, untouched by the sun.
For where the moon does shine
And shadows thrive
The sun should never touch at the same time.
It has no purpose.
Even the rain
Cold, damp and unpleasant,
Serves to bring life,
And rejuvenate the parched earth.
But the moon,
It does nothing but hide,
And plot, and scheme, and tinker,
To blot out the sun.
To eclipse it, if only for a moment,
And protect the planet.

The sun
Warm; bright,

Burning; dazzling,
Scorching; blinding.
Powerful and deceiving.
So toxic, so harsh,
Torching the planet, cracking the land.
Until it's only reprieve
From the vexing heat,
Is the soft, delicate caress of the darkness
Or the gentle, tender kiss of the night.
Yet still, the moon's love goes unnoticed...

... Or so we think.
If only we dared look closer...
Isn't it funny, how darkness
Is never seen without light?
And warmth without cold?
They dance along separate circles,
With a hop, skip and a jump.
Complimenting each other,
Too close, their circles break;
Too far and they cannot be seen.
Lovers doomed apart by the universe,

So they admire each other from afar,
Waiting for their paths to cross,
So the moon can feel the sun's
Passionate kiss once more,
If only for a moment.

Kayla Moerman (14)

Corona Cannot Even Begin To Imagine...

Imagine.
Had you just left,
Packed your bags, stopped the mortal theft,
But your insatiable, like a hungry storm,
That relentlessly bashes our towns leaving us broken and torn,
Imagine.
If you could've at least been just,
But only the vulnerable drive your lust,
They're the ones you mangled to dust.

Imagine.
Had you felt any regret, guilt, or shame - not at all!
You're suffocating us under your bloody pall,
Like a gluttonous grizzly that devours the east,
Leaving the west for his next feast.

Can you imagine the destruction you cause?
Would it hurt to just stop? And pause,
Because of you just going to the shop is now a suicide mission,
We beg of you: please stop and listen!
Do you know how we're terrified to embrace our own
Because we're scared we'll bring the murder weapon into their own homes?

And do you realise what happens to those you've slashed,
The ones in ITU who lie with their minds gashed?
Their lungs tired and sore,
But still, you attack them more and more.

So, can you imagine what we'll do to you,
Don't worry Corona, you'll get your due,
Redemption is no longer an option we can give,
We were stupid to think you would've let us live,
You will see how easily we crush your fake success
Go back to Lucifer and confess,
That you could never break the world at its worst,
2020 will not let you take us first.

Aiza Qayyum

A World Of Our Dreams

Imagine a sky, clear, bright blue,
Children, above the clouds, who flew,
Maybe a dessert made of icing and cake,
Such wonders my mind does shake.

Imagine if clouds danced like fire,
Bright sun blew down like a hairdryer,
Tiny trains choo-chooing as if to say hi,
Birds spread the news while passing by.

Imagine if spring flowers grew in a flash,
And autumn leaves blushed red abashed,
Summer brightens not frightens like a lamp,
And winter's blanket came down and damp.

Imagine new cool experiences every blink,
Every fault a mind quickly alters and kinks,
Focus building, learning as fast as sound
The places we could go infinite, unbound.

Imagine fresh water that never ran out,
Food not making Mother Nature pout,
Hunger vanished, every soul well cared,
World's wealths and beauties equally shared.

Imagine the world's surface left untouched,
Vast forests with their lush trees clutched,

White ice covering north, not melting away,
Keeping all our harmful, selfish acts at bay.

Imagine a world of endless peace and love,
Bonding like the threads of a woollen glove,
All creatures from fungi to animals to plants,
Working together, clearing each others' rants.

Imagine if scary darkness was never a thing,
If only light and good would prevail and sing,
Would it make this world a wonderful place,
Or would the good begin to lose its face?

Tanish Kirodian

Life Is Important

Man will implode and destroy every living thing on the earth...
The thing is, that will happen one day.
We will still blame some incompetent young person, who will push the button and eventually Earth will be non-existent.
Until another planet is born, here we are, writing the same thing again, taking no responsibility.
Let me take you back, let me take you way back, to the time the first wild flowers were born.
They filled the air with love, scent and oxygen.
The Mesozoic period brought a complete diversity of life forms,
we would not recognise now, such as the dinosaurs.
Squirrels of today, are the tiny shadow of the T-rex,
their little hands with four claws and the position of their dainty arms.
We try to reflect on the past but we do not realise the clues from the past are all around us, in every living form.
A squirrel dies and becomes something to feed nature's so many life forms.
But before a man dies, he somehow finds nature's heart.
He uses this knowledge to his advantage.
He uses it to become more powerful and to control nature and every living thing on Earth.
Man chops nature down, slowly squeezing out and strangling lives, murdering.
He is doing this now and nature is gasping and choking.

Man will replace it with something more disappointing. But what if we don't destroy, we nurture?

Sophie Hanif (11)

If We Were All The Same

Imagine... if we were all the same
The same birthday
The same problems
The same ideas and dreams

The world would count as one person only.
Everyone goes to the same hairdressers.
Everyone plays the guitar
No one is special.

Imagine... if one day a girl came into your classroom or office.
Everyone would stare at her until the sun burned their eyes.
It would be because she was different.
She had green eyes whilst everyone else's held blue.
She had a black folder whilst everyone else had a brown briefcase.

Her accent was unique and her shoes were different in size.
For the first time in history someone didn't fit in.
She was beautiful. But no one cared.
She had the richest laugh. But no one joined her.

On the biggest day of the year she would be the only one not having birthday cake.
A sad smile endorsed on her face.
Soon it was a scar.

And not even a cool one.
But instead cold.

She was famous
But no one even knew her name.
Not even me.

But where did she come from?
When asked she would say the world of imagining.
Where everyone was different and people were sometimes mocked for it.
Just like she was there.

That world is here.
We are the imagining world.
For we build rockets and phones.
We dream big long nights.
But we also mock.
So next time you laugh or blame at someone for being different.
Imagine being her...

Isla Caulfield (12)

Imagine If...

Imagine if you had one wish
Imagine if everyone wished for the same thing
Would it happen?

Imagine that there is no more starvation
People no longer go to bed feeling hungry
Children no longer wondering when their next meal is
Parents not worried that their children might die this minute from lack of nutrition
And that the farmers get paid what they earned
Instead of doing all the work and only getting paid a minuscule amount

Imagine that there are no millionaires
No more people who flaunt their money showing it off
If those rich people did some good and donated it to help charities or to homeless people
Not keep it for themselves
Imagine if those people helped

Imagine if we stopped climate change
The new generation and the old
Coming together to combat something which affects everyone
That all countries turned eco-friendly
And people helped the world instead of destroying it

Imagine if we helped homeless people get back on their feet
Don't treat them as if they're nothing,
One day that could be you
Treat them how you would want to be treated

Imagine if all this was possible
By working together and making a change
All it takes is for one person to change then the others will follow
Together we can help improve people's lives
Together we can help make their dream come true.

Bethany Milner

Imagine The Wars Others Have Been Through

Imagine the wars others have been through,
Not just the bombs and the guns,
The stress and hidden problems too,
Not being able to have fun.

A cry for help but it can't be heard,
Lost in their own dark mind,
Nobody understands their problems, not a word,
At least that's what depression feels like inside.

It gets so bad they can't look at themself,
They worry so much they lose focus,
They put everything before mental health,
Anxiety can't be fixed with a hocus pocus.

That one comment, you think it won't matter,
But it can push people over the edge,
Just because of their colour, you make them shatter,
Happiness going down faster than a child on a sledge.

Nothing ever revealed,
They're too afraid to turn the pages,
They keep the truth shut away, sealed,
Victims of abuse live their lives in cages.

Boom! Crash! The only two sounds,
They must have thought they couldn't do it anymore,
I can't imagine the things the soldiers have found,
I can't even begin to describe what it's like in a war.

Then there are the wars that come after the battle,
The trauma, the flashbacks, the things you can't believe are true,
It can all come back from the flick of a switch to the noise of the cattle,
Imagine the wars others have been through…

Aimée Richardson (13)

Imagine A World Where Animals Are In Charge

Imagine a world where humans are slaves,
To the great beasts that dwell under the waves.
Imagine a world where humans understand,
The majestic creatures that live on land.

Who would be the leader though?
The lion, the whale or even a flamingo.
Would there be tribes or would they live in unity?
In one great big old community

They would probably hate us a lot
For all of the destruction they got.
Such as all of their food and their woods
They probably think we're no good.

I think it would be scary,
To be slaves to those who are hairy.
I think it would be frightening,
To be slaves to those that move like lightning.

Just imagine being a pet
To a little old ferret
Kept in a little cave
With little room to bathe

Do you think they'll be kind and caring?
Or brave, bold, and daring?
Or will they be loud and vicious?
And think of us as delicious

Will they work us hard and long?
Snarling at us all night long
Or will they be fair and just,
And give us lots of trust?

The TV says that they are smart
And that they don't like our art.
They also think we're silly
For having so many lilies

I think I'd prefer if they left us alone
But then we steal from them to make it our own.
I for one like things the way they are
But how about you, would you like them in charge?

Tomisin Shaun Awofisayo

If Feelings Could Talk

If feelings could talk,
If they could speak without a breath leaving your mouth,
If they could scream without any air slipping through your lips,
If they could screech their gruesome words,
If they could purr their soothing letters,
If they could scratch into your skin,
If they could smooth over your burns;

If feelings could talk,
They would project themselves for everyone to hear,
They would blast themselves into every hidden corner of the room,
You would become vulnerable to their honesty.
You would become exposed to their harsh reality.

If feelings could talk,
Feelings would utter soft curses.
Feelings would whisper bitter blessings.
They would create wounds.
They would heal battle scars.

If feelings could talk,
I would savour their ugly voices,
Like a child savours a sweet on their tongue.
If feelings could talk,

I would take in their delicate beauty,
Like someone who smokes inhaling nicotine.

If feelings could talk,
I would feel each letter of their heartbreaking words,
I would feel every fibre of me break as the truth of them smacks the air.

If feelings could talk,
I would absorb each loving word,
I would let them consume me so I could hold their precious power.

Imagine.
Imagine if feelings could talk.
What a wonderful, disgusting mess it would create.

Abigail Edwards (17)

Imagine This

Imagine we never had two eyes to see
Imagine there was no such thing as me
Imagine we never had two ears to hear
Imagine there was no such thing as fear
Who would we be?

Imagine there were no trees for us to breathe
Imagine all of this would soon leave
Imagine there were no voices for us to scream
Imagine all of this was a dream
How would life seem?

Imagine there was no such thing as Earth
Imagine there was no such thing as birth
Imagine we never had to give
Imagine we never had anyone to be with
Where would we live?

Imagine we never had no hands to feel
Imagine none of this was real
Imagine we had no feet to walk
Imagine none of us could talk
What would this seal and what would it reveal?

Imagine we could live forever
Imagine we were always together
Imagine we could never lie

Imagine we could always fly
When would we say why?

Imagine we already knew all the solutions
Imagine the world was one big institution
Imagine everyone had good intentions
Imagine no one gave objections
Why would we then need to ask questions?

Imagine the sky wasn't blue
Imagine the clouds weren't white
Imagine the grass wasn't green
Imagine there was no night

Just imagine all of this
There's still so much more
You may not be able to...
Imagine!

Alimah Dugbartey (13)

My Journey To Being Enough

When I stand my thighs touch,
And then I wonder why I don't make you blush
Stretch marks cover my skin,
I just wish I could be thin

I throw coins in a wishing well,
But my stomach only seems to swell
Teardrops cover my face,
When will I find my place?

I'd be prettier if I lost weight,
Maybe that will someday be my fate
I starve myself and then I binge,
Why does my body have to whinge?

When will I be enough?

Six months later
I look in the mirror and feel disgust,
They say someday I will turn into dust
Now I'm in ED recovery,
This isn't what I thought it was, so lovely
I wish I could go back

I have no breasts and my thighs are wimpy
My period doesn't come

Can it be undone?
Skelton and bones is all that remains
Look what I did, I gave my life away
For what?
Not a single blood clot
Anorexia and then bulimia is all that has become of me,
I wish I could be
... Happy

When will I be enough?

Eight months later,
I'm free
And now I can just be,
I'm no longer in starvation or shoving fingers down my throat,
Yes, I may bloat

After all this time,
I can finally see why
I'm beautiful in my own way
And today, nothing you say
Will persuade me of any other way
As you don't know my story
Or any of my newfound glory.

Summer Higgs (12)

Thorns Or Flowers?

Imagine if there weren't any thorns,
No pain or hatred
And only flowers blossoming everywhere;
Life would sit in tranquillity
Love overpowering despair

Flora cannot choose where it grows
But it can choose how it grows;
Their beauty can still shine from the rubble
Even in frosty weather flowers can appear
But it's down to belief
To make the path ahead seem clear,

Yet the enticing, beautiful flora are like humans
Taking their time to grow,
The things around them
Don't dictate their potential -
Flowers can bloom wonderfully
With a little luck and strength

In tranquil places
Vivid colours adorn the petals,
Like warm smiles on faces

However in dispirited places
Thorns will appear,

In dark places
Lurks hidden fear

Imagine the world showed all of its flowers
And got rid of all its thorns,
Wrath and hatred shouldn't exist
Instead the sun should shine
Vanquishing the mist

So don't be afraid to show your flowers,
The flowers purify the path ahead;
Take time to adopt and grow your flowers
and to dispatch the thorns that cause agony

Let your colours run wild,
Let them grow tall and vast
Resembling only you,
Don't let the thorns pierce your life
For if we truly believe - the flowers will always bloom.

Reana Lata (12)

A Canvas

Imagine the world a canvas...
Would painting it be worth it?
Would you paint it blue
Where we don't have a clue?
Or a fiery red,
Where we fight instead?
With bows and arrows,
Amidst fires and under sunsets

What about a delicious yellow?
You coward, add some flowers,
Make it sweet and sour! Don't let your fellows cower!
Find a mellow cello,
Make it play 'Othello'!
Add some evil spray!
Oh no! Wait!
Run, you're a prey!

What about a rich purple?
Where we dance and tingle?
Peekaboo,
It's time to mingle!
Party and Pringles!

How about a dash of black?
Money, fame and power brag!
Oh, I know! A simple green!

But will you be so kind and keen?
Or perhaps only black and white.
C'mon, you know what I'm talking about.

I see a blissful brown!
Bear hugs, baths and crowns!
A sprinkle of pink?
Puberty?
Pimples?
No, it stinks!
Midnight grey!
Nuh-uh. It'll make you sway...
Now that we've reached the end...
Will you leave it as it is
Or will you let your imagination run wild, colouring it as you want!

Abby M (17)

Liberation

Imagine a world where you feel safe to walk alone,
A world in which there is no fear of being followed home,

Imagine a world where rape wasn't justified by what the victim decided to wear,
A world where tight trousers weren't the cause of treatment so unfair,

Imagine a world where girls weren't taken out of a school situation,
A world where their length of skirt mattered less than their education,

Imagine a world where sanitary items were a necessity,
Where events weren't missed due to a time of tensity,

Imagine a world where historical women were deemed as important to learn about as men,
Where in literature you read books by sharp-minded ladies as well as the ones written by a male pen,

Imagine a world where men can be the victims of sexism too,
Where they can also face prejudice that makes them feel blue,

Imagine a world where a woman controls her own body and has the right to be free,
Where abortion is universally legal, is this not how it should be?

This is the world I want; a better place to be,
But what makes me the saddest of all is that it's a place I will most likely never see...

Maegan Sharp (16)

True Story

Picture the scene,
your home village in Afghanistan,
you're just trying to hang out with your mates,
playing football like a mad man.
But suddenly there are explosions,
and your ears are ringing like they are broken,
and during all the commotion,
you see more blood than the Pacific Ocean.
Your best mate is completely dead,
but that's not the worst to be said.
a gang pulls up firing shots,
one for your bro and one for your head.
But somehow you manage to escape,
run to your home where it's meant to be safe,
but your family is all dead,
everywhere is just bloodshed.

With just a toothbrush, clothes and a fake passport,
you make it to a boat port,
still teardrops falling from your face,
you decide to run somewhere safe,
you hear the UK is a better place,
your life tangled like a shoelace.

Now you're in the back of a lorry,
it stops at Dover border,

no documents to show in order,
you are now suffering a stress disorder.

So British customs gives you to the Home Office,
thankfully they let you stay,
though your life is still grey,
it will be brighter another day.
Now all you can do is pray,
appreciate every opportunity that comes your way,
to try to reorder your life
and bring back all the light.

Aman Saleem

Imagine Where...

Imagine a place where humans were extinct
Imagine a place where nobody blinked
Imagine a place where all things were immortal
Imagine a place where there was a portal
That took you to a place where dreams came true

Imagine a place where everyone flew
Imagine a place where cows were pink
Imagine a place where a pig could wink
Imagine a place where everybody was equal

Imagine a place where you could jump in a computer game
Imagine a place where there was no one to blame
Imagine a place where you only had one wish
Imagine a place where stars were gold-ish

Imagine a place where kids ruled the world
Imagine a place where the flowers twirled
Imagine a place where we could change history
Imagine a place where there were mysteries

Imagine a place where people knew the real you
Imagine a place where the wind blew
Upwards

Imagine a place where we were just avatars in a game
Imagine a place where there was no shame

Imagine a place where everyone was fair
Imagine a place where we all learned to share

Imagine a place where nobody was wrong
Imagine a place where I could stay all day long
Imagine a place where you didn't have to say goodbye
But do not sigh
Just *imagine!*

Amirah Akter (11)

Imagine A Kind Society

Imagine a world where everyone was treated the same,
Imagine if the only struggles were cooking and cleaning.
Imagine a life where no matter who you were, you were loved, and you knew it.

Imagine if everyone loved you for who you were.
You could do everything you wanted to do without people saying that you couldn't.
You didn't have to be size 8 to be a model,
You didn't have to be pretty to be famous.
You didn't get bullied for being different.

The more we sit and imagine this society,
The less possible it is to be created.
So, let's start right now.

Instead of killing someone,
Give them a hug.
Instead of hurting them,
Handshake them.

Do you know that girl who always sits by herself at lunchtime?
You can sit with her; she might need someone to talk to.
Remember that elderly lady who you saw struggling to carry her shopping bags?
Next time, you could go and help her.

Remember that boy who cried and you laughed at him?
He is slowly losing his relatives.
Remember that old man who you made fun of for the ugly scars?
He fought for our country.

Don't judge people before you get to know them.
Instead of imagining a kind world, let's create one!

Maisy-Ilar Moazzenkivi (13)

The Day Everyone Goes Away

Football in my hands to find someone to play
Asked all my family and here's what they had to say...
Mom said: "Not right now, need to do the laundry"
Little brother said: "Not right now, I need to go to pee"
Dad said: "Not right now, I need to get some gas"
Older sister said: "Not right now, stick that football up your a**!"
So today was the day,
I wished my entire family away.

At first it made me feel like a king,
I could have danced on the rooftops and made the birds sing,
Going out in the sunshine, I played on my DS outside,
No one made me take a break; they just let it slide,
Chocolates, sweets, crisps, all I ate.
After all, who was there to berate?
Here I was by myself and alone...
Wait up, hold the phone

Alone? No, not alone but lonely

Fear made me weep and weep and weep,
Until I could cry no more,
I shuddered as lightning struck outside,

Making me feel so small
If only my parents were here for a cuddle,
Or my siblings to hide under the bed.
If only... but they're not here.
My fault; I wished them away.

Who in the world would want to be me?
When I feel incredibly lonely.

Amy Cassidy (16)

Free To Dream

I have something to tell you

From the moment you start school
People expect you to be cool
But that's not true
They don't make the rule

Imagine a world where
You are free to be you without judgement
Where you can walk without the constant glare
Where you can talk without the whispers

Imagine a world
Where bullying is not a thing
Where you're not constantly crying in secret
Where you feel safe to live

Imagine a world
Where your colour doesn't make people stare
Where your colour doesn't cause people fear
Where you're free to go anywhere

Imagine a world
Where girls aren't constantly living in fear
Where human trafficking, rape and abuse aren't a norm
Where an eighteen-year-old isn't forced to marry

Imagine a world
Where we don't lose sight of who we are
Where we can shine like a binary star
Where society doesn't dictate our lives

Imagine a world where
I can be free to dream
I can be me, my colour, my race
I can be treated equally

Can you see it?

It's a whole new world
So, hold onto it and never let go
Be free to dream of that place
Be free to venture into a whole new world.

Chizitere Ofurum (18)

Imagine If We Are Just Characters Living In A Simulation?

Imagine if we are just characters in a simulation,
Mindless robots inhabiting a fake world.
Living a lie every day,
With no clue on how to escape.

Who is controlling us?
Making our every single move.
Is it 'the man', 'the government'?
Distracting us so we don't find out the exposing truth.

Who are we?
Identities lost like meaningless tiny little specks in the universe.
Brainwashed to complete missions in this game called life.
Are the relationships we form over time even real?
Do the doctrines we are made to believe even matter?

Who is watching us?
Are they watching us like how we watch TV?
This was all part of the plan written in codes and algorithms,
Being commanded like pawns in a game of chess.

Imagine if we are just characters in a simulation,
Mindless robots inhabiting a fake world.
Living a lie every day,
With no clue on how to escape.
Are we in too deep or do we just have to look at things at a different angle...?

Aleema Mirza Hamid (14)

Imagine - A Tranquil Ocean

Imagine a world without difficulty,
I know it might be quite hard to see,
A world with no war,
No thunder crashing the walls,
Just us living in tranquillity.

Close your eyes,
This might be hard but try,
Imagine a world without destruction or crime,
Without innocent people having to hide,
Without the harmony of children's pleads and cries.

Now open your eyes,
Our world is an ocean,
Filled with pollution.

We play predator and prey,
We make tsunamis and waves,
But don't forget the beautiful things we create.

Those innocent people fight for their rights,
Others give up their time so the children don't cry,
We educate those youths so they don't start gang fights.
All I can say is at least some try.

We have harsh waves and smooth ripples,
An okay day filled with troubles,
We neither upgrade nor downgrade.

Imagine our ocean without fear or pain,
Wouldn't it be such a beguiling wave?

Rhianna Adams (13)

Imagine If You Could Control Time

Imagine if you could control time,
All you do is simply just think,
And then the world around you stops,
Instantly and all in sync.

But you can also rewind or fast forward,
Travel to the past or skip to the future,
Experience all the greats that have concluded,
And all the innovations that are to come.

Imagine if you could control time,
Unlimited knowledge without reading a word,
A life-saver without any skill,
So much power and greatness with just one feat.

But with power comes responsibility, right?
So I ask you, how will you use this ability,
Surely you could pause time and go around helping others,
Or will you use this stillness and serenity to satisfy yourself?

Imagine if you could control time,
So many instances in history that ultimately ended in disaster,
All could be erased with your mind,
Only requires energy and ironically a lot of your time.

To be honest though you don't need to,
You don't need to try to be a Good Samaritan,
Let's be real, no one will ever know,
But you will, you will know if you did the right thing.

Mithran Loganathan (14)

Imagine, Wish And Pray

Imagine if my wishes were fulfilled
that's enough to make any soul thrilled

"What's your wish?" you might say
well, I imagine, wish and pray

For the end of poverty
which is an ancient calamity

I wish for the end of wars
for the end of criminals behind bars

I wish for an erasement of racism
sexism, ageism and classism

For the end of xenophobia
and don't forget Islamophobia

I pray for the demise of global warming
many times we've received a warning

That our Earth is dying
even though there are people out there trying

Prepossessing animals are dying out
can you imagine the Earth without

Creatures
With stunning, breathtaking features?

I imagine a solution
to air, water and land pollution

But do not lose hope
there is still a rope
that we can hang on to and cope

So together we say
"Imagine, wish and pray!"

Abdurrahman Hussein (15)

The Question No One Can Seem To Answer

It's as if yesterday we were making daisy chains
and now we're just trapped by chains
it's as if we wanted to grow up
and now we would love to rewind the clock

Why does everything change?
Why does everything have to change?
Why can't life be still for a moment?
No movement, no sound, not even the sound of the wind, or leaves rustling

Just still

Can you hear that?
Nothing
absolutely nothing
and for a moment we are still and calm

And then life resumes
like it always does
swirling us up in whatever direction it pleases
like swimming against the harshest of waves

... Drowning
... Drowning

... Sinking
... Alive

Why are we here?
What do we take away from this 'great experience'
and what do we give to it?
Do we just waste these lives questioning, or do we waste
them not questioning enough?

What is time?
Is it just a mere idea to make us feel safer?
Is everything already planned out?
What do we have control over?

So what is life?
Does anyone have any idea
or is it just the question no one can seem to answer?

Inderpreet Kaur (15)

The Wolf

Sharp eyes
of which can break your shy expression
with only a nervous glance

Delicate grey fur
of which can turn you naive
with its innocent appearance

Bloodthirsty teeth
of which can rip you apart
but yet they don't

Never again will it see its pack
its family
as it wanders alone
now with only its instincts to follow

Young and vulnerable
the calm, unprotected creature
walks silently along a winding path

Beyond the mist is a girl
she is not special
she is but the same as you and I

But yet she doesn't stop
not when she sees the creature
nor when she knows the instincts of this young mammal

She waits
the lonely animal now running
chasing in her direction

She waits for it to come
and even then does the girl
stare at the innocence
the vulnerability of this young creature

Only then does the girls walk
she walks towards what we now know is a wolf
and with mighty force
the girl leaps
and her hallucinations arise
as there is no wolf

Only her innocence
her vulnerability
her alone once again.

Phoebe Allington (12)

Change

Imagine if you were the only person on Earth.
With the whole planet in your hands.
Lost in the vastness.
Engrossed in your thoughts,
Feelings and suddenly
You can see everything.
The history of the world swarming around you
Memories, wars, hardship.
You can see it all.
The hungry children, the melting ice, the ruthless, selfish egos.
The betrayal of humankind, the loss of homogeneity.
The money-hungry losing sight of life.
The wars, genocides and pure abhorrence.
With the blood of the innocent on their hands.
The moral compass, abandoned;
And here you are.
Surrounded by it all.
What would you have done?
Would you have given those forbidden to speak a voice
Or given the bitterly hungry food?
Allowed everyone to feel wanted,
Needed and loved?
What would you have done?
Now in the midst of solitude,
If you had the power,

Over this planet, seeing it,
Would you save it?

Avneet Hayer (14)

Imagine If We Could Talk To God

Imagine if we could talk to God:

Our life will have a bad turn,
As we must sometimes learn.
We think we are free to fly,
But fear to touch the sky.
Talk to God every day and night,
Who will show you a path to fight.

We think we will win in everything,
But we are unable to achieve anything.
As we are ready to quit,
When hard times hit.
But talk to God who would say,
Bad days will fly away.

We all have lots of problems to think about,
But we should never break out.
Never give up,
As you will win the golden cup.
Just imagine we can talk to God again,
Who knows your pain.

Your victory might be slow,
But one day you will glow.

We hold everything inside,
But why hide?
Talk to God who knows you deep,
Who says good thoughts is what you should keep.

We have lots of problems to face,
But life is a race.
Your new beginning,
Is the key to winning.
Imagine you could talk to God,
Who says everything happens for the good.

Imagine if we could talk to God,
All our problems will be solved by God.

Thenuya Chandrasegaran (16)

Bullying

Imagine being called names,
And excluded from games,
I've been deprived of my rights,
And forced into fights.

Imagine going on your phone,
But they follow you like a drone,
They say hurtful things online,
And threaten to break my spine.

Imagine telling someone,
About everything they've done,
They get in trouble,
But they return as a double.

Imagine having enough,
You show that they're not so tough,
You get your hands dirty and show that you're mad,
But you get penalised and look really bad.

Imagine having no friends,
Your torture has no ends,
When you really need someone,
They say, "Just ignore it, young one!"

Imagine wanting to leave,
And more conspiracies begin to weave,

Don't want a superhero or a preacher,
But just a brave and no-nonsense teacher.

Imagine one day if they come back to their senses,
Seeing their attitude and their offences,
And apologise for the hurt they have caused,
Deliberating on the outcome, if they had just paused.

Abhishek Rajan (14)

If I Won The Lottery

If I won the lottery:
Well, where would I start?
Creating world peace,
That would be an important part!

I can't say I could fix everything
The process may be slow
I would try and spread laughter, love and happiness
I would really give it a go!

I would raise awareness of global warming
To show the planet that we care
Make everyone think long and hard
That for the future generations we must prepare

I would give every child a warm home
No one should be in poverty
I'd give them a laptop and hot food
This is fundamentally important to me

I would buy a plethora of COVID vaccines
To protect and preserve life
So when it is eliminated
The world will light up without strife

This year has been a strange one
But one in which we have all grown

I think we have learnt so much
That with our families we are never alone

So if I won the lottery:
I would have definitive, grandiose plans
But not of fortunes or material things
Of using it wisely, with healing hands.

Ralph James Gilroy (12)

If Things Were Different

Imagine we were all equal,
Imagine we were all the same,
Imagine we lived in a different world,
Imagine life was a game.

Imagine if we had one wish,
Imagine if we could control our thoughts,
Imagine there was no negativity,
We would be capable of all sorts.

Mental health is no laughing matter,
Especially in this day and age,
We're constantly bringing each other down,
Feeling like we are trapped in a cage.

We live in a messed up society,
Full of hatred, judgements and fights,
But imagine we all walked together
Into this little ray of light.

Just imagine things were different,
And life didn't pass us by,
We should treasure every memory,
Before it's time to fly.

Imagine if everyone was accepted,
Imagine the only thing this world could see

Is lots of laughter and joy,
Filled with love and positivity.

Lucy Walton (15)

Tears From The Sky

I grew from a seed, a normal seed.
And now I know that I couldn't be freed
So that must be why,
Tears came from the sky.

I had a plan all along,
To escape where I belonged.
I sadly watched my leaves fly away,
Whilst I stayed here for another day.

I was then a sapling, a normal sapling,
And now I know that I could not have gone travelling.
So that must be why,
Tears came from the sky.

As I got older,
My attempts then got bolder;
I waved around my branches,
Trying to increase my chances.

Then along came grandmother, with a young, little Lucy,
They said that they'd just been to see a movie.
They saw branches flailing in the air,
And on their faces was a look of care.

Now I'm a fully grown tree, with Lucy still by me,
She talks to me and laughs with glee.

I've watched her play and grow,
In wind, rain, sun and snow.

I grew from a seed, a normal seed.
And now I know, how to be freed
So that must be why,
No tears come from the sky.

Harry Parsons (12)

If The World Ended Tomorrow

Imagine if the world ended tomorrow
Where would you live, what would you do and who would you meet?
If you went skiing on a mountain,
Would you build a snowman?
Would you live there for a day?
At the top would you scream hip hip hooray?

If the world ended tomorrow
What would you see, how old would you be, where would you go?
Would you go to the top of the mountain
To go see the yeti family
Or harvest sweet peas?

If the world ended tomorrow
What would you be or even who?
Would you like to be a yeti too?

Imagine if the world ended tomorrow
You could go to the zoo
If you went there who would you take?
Would you go see the elephants and the snakes?
You could take your mum then what could you do?

You could have a nice spa day
Or stick things with glue!

If the world ended tomorrow
How would you take this news?
Would you take your belongings everywhere,
Or hand them to people in need?

Imagine if the world ended tomorrow...
What would you do?

Rebecca Cronin

Invisible

I wave
I jump
I scream
No one seems to notice me
Is it true?
Is it real?
I really can't believe
All these years of hiding in the shadows
Disappearing in the crowd
No one noticed,
No one knew - I never made a sound
Now I stand here appalled and dismayed
Knowing what I had done
I stood in the shadows for too long
And now I'm totally gone

Should I feel sad?
Should I feel happy?
I really cannot tell
But my insides spin and spin
Making me rethink,
I feel disordered
Replaced
And can't flash a grin

Now I'm completely imperceptible
And no one can tell it's me
My infinitesimal amount of friends
And my 'loving' family

Don't believe permanence lasts
Permanence is indefinite
Temporary beyond belief.
You can never tell how long you last
And how long you disappear
But here I am
Invisible to the eye
And trust me it is no lie
How long I've been gone is a mystery
But then again who would actually miss me?

Aaishah Niqheth Salahudeen (12)

Adventure

Imagine a world of adventure,
One where you can discover.
Imagine a world of magic,
One where you can be anything!

You could go beyond the ordinary human life,
Be unique.
You could do anything,
Be free!

Imagine a world of adventure,
One where you can have fun.
Imagine a world of magic,
One where you can toy with dreams.

You could go beyond the definition of 'amusement',
Create something new.
You could forge a longing,
Create a dream.

Imagine a world of adventure,
One where you can divulge.
Imagine a world of magic,
One where you can experiment.

You could go beyond your life,
And find secrets.

You could try new things
And never get it wrong!

Imagine a world of adventure,
One where you can discover.
Imagine a world of magic,
One where you can manipulate.

You could go beyond your bedroom window,
Unravel the beauty of life!
You could form wreathes of creativity,
Unravel the never-ending thrill of imagination.

Jannat Burgaz (13)

Imagine A World

Imagine a world without war,
Where people could walk without fear,
And there was no violence or gore,
No one was abused or refused,
Imagine a world where people were equal.

Imagine a world where you weren't judged,
For the colour of your skin,
Or the person you love,
No segregation, or discrimination,
Imagine a world where you could be who you wanted.

Imagine a world without climate change,
Where the rainforests still stood strong,
The air didn't choke you and the ocean life wasn't gone,
No extinction or pollution,
Imagine a world where we cared for the planet.

Imagine a world where everyone was safe,
Where people would listen,
And no one felt like they had to escape,
Or were trapped in sadness,
No isolation, or violation,
Imagine a world where mental health mattered.

Imagine if this was reality,
And the world wasn't corrupted

But sadly this isn't true,
And nothing was disrupted.

Grace Betteridge (12)

The Corruption Of Our Society

Money is no longer just a currency.
It is also our pride.
The money that we gamble with,
The money that we sleep with,
The money that has taken over our lives.

Wealth has become a competition.
A race to become the filthiest,
A race to see who can survive.

We have always dreamed about power, not knowing the nightmares that come with it.
The corruption of our government running to 'try' keep our economy fit.
It is never a yes or no answer, it has either a yes or a yes.

A free-will country?
Yet the prejudice we cannot forget.

George Floyd, Breonna Taylor, Elijah McClain.
May their souls rest.
I could name so many more,
Yet the world will not show remorse.

More than five million Muslims in camp and yet the world is still,

Silent.

History is repeating itself,
Except there is no war.
Unless there is.
A war between ourselves.
A war between yourselves.

Is this how our future will be?

Ayeza Siddiqui (14)

Imagine If This War Was A Dream

We prepare in our friend's secret base,
And make our way to the battlefield,
We march towards the land we fight for,
There is nothing me and my friends want more,
Arrows rain upon the enemy's side,
Many of the men have started to die,
Imagine the land we fight for,
If we all supported the same cause.

We find and overthrow a tyrant,
And now I have it all again,
But I realise it is not my time,
And I pass my power away,
My friend now rules over our land,
But before our final victory,
We have no idea who the traitor will be.

We find ourselves running away,
As our land blows up and fades away,
The chaos of the war starts to increase,
As the traitor spawns into two beasts,
And we fight them till they are no more.

The chaos ends, now we live in peace,
The rebuilding starts, in honour of the deceased,

But there is one thing we don't know,
Was this whole war just a dream?

Summaiyya Khatun (14)

Imagine Living In Your Head

Imagine you can't read, you can't write,
You can't scream, you can't fight.
Day after day you stay put,
You wish you could just wiggle your foot.

Imagine you can't laugh, you can't talk,
You can't stand, you can't walk,
Day after day you still try,
As you hear everybody else walk by.

You want to tell everyone what you feel,
You want to be able to feel real.
You feel like you are stuck in your own head,
You know you will never leave this bed.

Imagine you feel invisible, you feel so weak,
You want to be able to play games like hide-and-seek.
You can hear the beeps from the machine,
Every day is the same routine.

What are trains? What are whales?
What are planes? What are snails?
Questions spin round and round in your head;
You feel like you would rather be dead.

This may just be your imagination,
But it's someone else's situation.

Sian Baldwin (13)

Soon? Soon

Let me pitch to you a world
which you might recognise;
no graphs, pie charts or men in suits to sell it to you,
just imagine.

A world where
you have to wear a mask
only to hide your emotions,
pretend you like the gift.

A world where,
three's a crowd
is nothing more than a social euphemism,
encouraging the intimacy found
in isolation,

not a rule of law.

A world where,
the irresponsibility of a busy beach
refers only to the mother whose son has
disappeared alone
over the dunes to get away from it all,
just the beach.

Can you imagine a world where
we eat out to help out

only ourselves because cooking is too much after
such a long week, month, year...

Are you smiling yet? Longing?
Eyes creasing and glistening?
We can't see your mouth through the fabric.

This world we can imagine,
because we had it, once.

And we'll see it again soon,
soon.

Abby Butler (17)

Imagine. Just Imagine...

Imagine.
A world where the houses are made of gingerbread and lollipops.
Where the streets are made of butterflies
And the walls are made of chocolate.
Imagine a world as sweet as mine.
Imagine.
Just imagine.

Imagine.
I want to imagine a world exactly like the ones van Gogh painted.
A unique world where even the greatest flaws are perfect.
Stretch marks.
Different bodies, different faces are perfect.
Freckles, big noses, long legs, short legs.
Everything.
A calm haven.
A safe space.
Imagine.
Just imagine.

Imagine.
Just imagine.
A world as sweet as cinnamon.
A world as sweet as candy.
Imagine.

The world to me is a black hole.
The same thing can draw you in, and it can also crush you
The only way to steer clear is to love yourself.
Once you learn that, imagine the power you wield within yourself.

Imagine.
Just imagine.

Elif Nisa (13)

What People Think

Imagine this...
What if I could hear what people think?
Would they be good thoughts, or bad?
Or have they been wondering if they should go to the ice rink?
For three hours!

Think about it...
Are they thinking to propose?
Or maybe to go shopping?
Or maybe they just want to pick their nose?
That's gross!

Maybe you don't want to know, but...
What if they think that you look great today?
Or maybe they like your new car?
Or maybe they just want to say...
Remember to pay and display!

So, in conclusion...
Should I hear what people think?
I'd know everything about them,
Their ups, their downs, and even their blinks,
So yes!

I'd love it...
I'd know if they like gaming or art,
Or if they hate mosquitoes,

Or if they are about to fart,
That would be fun!

"Eww, did he just fart?"
On second thoughts, maybe not!

Sarabdeep Bhatia (14)

Imagine... An Unrestricted World

Imagine a world without physical pain,
Emotional anguish, constant unease cannot reign,
Where financial hardships have no place to stay,
Where doubts and confusion are driven away,
Where every tear is drawn from every eye,
With no separation, no broken promises to rectify,
A place where nature is cherished and free,
Where stunning sights are what you yearn to see,
Where unexpected rainbows emerge from above,
Hopes and dreams soar as a delicate dove,
Buoyant birds of friendship glide endlessly,
Sparkling rivers chat among the dazzling sea,
Where all nations join in unity,
Growing and flourishing at each opportunity,
Where friends and family are embraced,
And masks and sanitizers are replaced,
With the hug of a child so appreciated,
And a cuppa together now eagerly anticipated,
Imagine the paradise now unfurled,
Imagine an unrestricted world.

Zara Hope Jones (12)

If I Had One Wish

If I had one wish,
I would be the richest 11-year-old in the world
If I had one wish,
I would cure Coronavirus and all other diseases around the world
If I had one wish,
I would be the fastest 11-year-old boy in the galaxy
If I had one wish,
I would be immortal just to see the evolution of all young writers
If I had one wish.
I would be the first black prime minister and make the United Kingdom a more inclusive country for all races
If I had one wish,
I would give people in different countries the same opportunity that I have
If I had one wish,
I would tackle poverty and homelessness
If I had one wish,
I would make kids rule the world
If I had one wish,
I would go back twenty years to see what the world was like
If I had one wish,
I would create peace in the world
If I had one wish, oh lord if I had one wish...

Desmond Jones (11)

Bad Blue Sunday

As I wake up my head feels dizzy,
Like I just got caught in a blizzy.
What a mysterious hospital to lie in,
The wind travelling like a flash.
I shiver as it passes me by in a dash,
Buildings floating as time loops,
The birds say meow and the cats say moo,
The sun is broken, its pieces falling down onto Earth,
While the moon is resetting its birth.
The clocks ticking but reversing,
Meteors raining but rebirthing.
I say to myself, "It cannot be!"
But my eyes respond with, "No, I see!"
The sky is dark and the clouds are raining toxic acid,
No people to be seen.
But buildings and meteors,
Life is a loop broken and blue on this blue Sunday
Today really is bad, what say you?

Ryan Arthur (11)

A Perfect World

Imagine, if the world was perfect...
No nook or cranny left imperfect.
No more hate or war and inequality, just love.
Or would it be disastrous?
Every day the same, no room for wrong.
What if someone was imperfect?
All of the 'what ifs' and 'I wonders' would they exist?
Or would it be: "This is the perfect way so stick to it, no questions asked?"
Sounds lovely doesn't it?
A perfect world, but think if the world was perfect, would what we think matter? Would we matter?
If the world was perfect, why would it need us? To run it?
It may need a few high leaders or rich people just so the world has purpose.
But the rest of us would have no use.
So be thankful for the perfectly imperfect world in which we live and matter.

Erin Marie Jones (13)

Imagine If I Could Be

Imagine if I could be a Christmas tree
How magical this would be

My coat of darkest forest green
At six foot tall so by all can be seen

My branches so glossy and perfectly formed
Upon which pretty decorations would be adorned

I would be dressed in tinsel and coloured lights
I would twinkle and sparkle all through the night

My wishes for baubles hand-made, memories or bought from abroad
I am a Christmas tree unique, nit themed, by my family adored

All the time when Christmas passes and my needles start to fall
I am stripped of baubles and lifted from the hall

I am put into my garden to grow in the sun and rain
To be ready for next winter, to bring joy once again.

Ella Harrison (12)

Imagine A Time

Imagine a time where we weren't treated differently because of our skin colour or by religion.
A time where everyone would love each other for who they were.
A time before this pandemic where we were all with friends and family enjoying, celebrating the times of our lives.
But instead we are having to isolate, stay home.
All this ran through us like a lightning bolt,
Day by day having to do what we are told and losing our loved ones in the process.
But imagine, imagine if this didn't happen,
What if we are all living a dream and this is just a test?
Imagine if the world was peaceful, no war, just peace.
But what can we do?
All we can do is imagine this in our minds
But could we make this a reality?

Maryam Hussain (16)

History: Now Imagine

Imagine if you and I were running barefoot, hunting with the cavemen and cavewomen in the Stone Age.
You and I could witness great things that happened in the past.
You and I could even change the past.
Great things we could do together like fight with the soldiers who bravely fought in World War I and II.
We would truly be proud to help those who were injured for they fought for us and they risked their lives
I would love to know how Isaac Newton felt when he found out about gravity.
It would be exciting to learn something that we may have not known without him.
Now it is time to go, it is time to tell you about the past
Eyes wide open in awe knowing what truly happened in the past,
Now just imagine if one day we could witness the future.

Jadesola Lanlokun (12)

Imagine...

Imagine the battle, the bloodshed, and tears,
Overwhelming the site of destruction and fear.

Imagine all the soldiers who could have made it home,
Lived a life, shared a smile, had a family of their own.

Imagine the terror when going out to fight,
Knowing very well this could be their last night.

Imagine all the longing to make it back alive,
Seeing Mother's face, only one more time.

Imagine her heart fading away,
As her son was lowered into his makeshift grave.

Imagine what would happen if humans weren't so cruel,
So filled with violence and a desire to rule.

So as this last gunshot rings in your ears,
Close your eyes,
Say a prayer,
And imagine a place called home...

Jannah Hussain (14)

Imagine

Imagine a world where everyone was the same
same nose, same eyes, same smile.
In every corner you take,
you see the same emotionless silhouette.
With every word you exchange,
you hear the same meaningless story.
You see no difference, you see no creativity, you see no diversity,
Small things, unnoticeable
like the way you face angles when you smile
is what makes you different.
Everyone is unique in their own way,
don't be ashamed of who you are,
let your colours shine.
Blind everyone with your confidence,
show them what you are.
Everyone has a story to tell,
make sure the world hears.
You only live once, show what you want to be remembered by.

Sarah Curticean (14)

Diversity

As diverse as it could get,
From those who we first met.
Never have we seen someone just the same,
Because everyone has a completely unique frame.

So many different cultures to list,
All of them so unique that you just had to insist.
Friends from different ethnicity groups, they all just came,
Never in a million years will you see someone just the same.

As diverse as it could get,
From those who we first met.
Something new is all you can say,
Everyone is unique in their own way.

Diversity is everywhere,
It is here and it is there.
Everyone equal but unique is something you should know,
You will see someone different again tomorrow.

Venisha Lobo (12)

Frosty Weather

Every wintry day that rolled by,
Was enough for white clouds to form in the sky.
Windows shut and locked tight,
To stop the icy-cold bite.
Some days it was so dark to make you lost,
And if you squint you can see blue or white frost.
As you pass the once boring undecorates houses,
And everywhere you can hear shouts.
The young cheerful children come out to play,
Making your heart feel warm every day.
The sun likes to hide its shine and covers itself behind clouds,
Covering away from the cold, but listening to the children who are loud.
Houses are decorated, red, blue, green,
They look lovely and fit for a queen.
The sound of doorbells being rung from visitors can be heard all over town,
And people pour in without frowns.

Hafsa Ahmed Bhatti

A Thought For Humanity

As we chase the blue marble
And cater to every petty need
There are screams, shrieks and let us not forget pleads
Of the oppressed.

You sit with your Midas touch
Not knowing when enough is enough
You beam with ignorance and pride
Because what difference does it make if millions die?

I sit alone and dwell
What could have been of humanity if we felt?
If we thought a bit more wiser and acted a bit more kinder?
Perhaps then the world would just be so much nicer

Let's scrap the imagination and the anticipation
And the dehumanisation and the indoctrination.
Instead
Let's ignite fire in our hearts
Let's burn serenity into our souls

So we can one day rejoice and sing
When humanity finds its heart again.

Tayba Mehrban (14)

Why?

Her eyes are stunning,
Big and bold,
Her luscious hair,
Are locks of gold.

But deep down inside,
She knows.

She knows that,
No one is equal,
Though they protest,
Colour, gender, everything matters,
This is what she detests,
But why should they?

In history class she learns,
That girls never once had a turn.
They have done extraordinary things yes,
And though they do their best.
But the spotlight won't shine on them in return.

She learns that a darker shade,
Will not fade,
And won't be the same,
Even with fame
And though they fight back,

They get attacked
Is history repeating itself?

Why does this matter,
Skin colour and gender,
She asks her teacher,
The teacher just shakes her head,

Why?

Ruchira Hariyapureddy

Imagine

I love the night,
It fills my soul,
If I had one wish it would be to keep it all,
The stars, the moon and even the light.
It is just the only thing that is right.

I would like to be in Russia,
And feel the dense wind upon my face.
I would like to feel the warmth of hot chocolate swirling down my throat at a slow pace.
I would like to glide my fingers against snow and drift my feet easily below.

I would like to be in a dream,
And float steadily in the air.
To see all the things around me and calmly just stare.
To do the unimaginable that can't be done on Earth.
And look at the things I have done right from birth.

Imagine like everything you have dreamt has come true.
Imagine it is up to you...

Tammy Oyebanji (11)

No Goodbyes

Many years ago when my soul still laughed,
And my happiness hadn't drowned in the bottomless bath,
And the ones I loved were still around,
And they had not been buried in the ground,

Imagine if they were still here,
To laugh and sing and drink good beer,
And to make me feel loved,
And not alone,
When they were right here,
In my home,

Imagine if they were on my phone,
Their minds uploaded,
Their kindness cloned,
Their cheeriness still around,
And their humour still edgy but very profound,

Imagine that your loved ones didn't die,
Or at least didn't go before their time,
And you didn't have arguments or foes,
But as they say,
You'll never feel high if you've never felt low.

Timothy Kennett (11)

Imagine If They Knew The Real You

Imagine if they knew the real you.
Hurting inside,
while they however just see a smile.
Imagine if they knew the real you.

Imagine if they knew the real you.
Shy and afraid,
not like the confident girl that is displayed.
Imagine if they knew the real you.

Imagine if they knew the real you.
Popular, many friends of your own
the truth is you're all alone.
Imagine if they knew the real you.

Imagine if they knew the real you.
Great at everything, always in a rush
but what if the pressure has become too much.
Imagine if they knew the real you.

Imagine if they knew the real you.
Don't be scared, tell the truth
I'm sure they'd see your point of view
Imagine if they knew the real you.

Emma Bronwen Lacey (13)

Imagine

Imagine we were pixel avatars
In a computer game
Would we walk, talk and move
Exactly the same?

Could we fly to the moon
With no protective gear
Or could we fight a big, scary dragon
Without any fear?

Could we be robots, unicorns and zombies too?
Could we be animals living in the zoo?
Could we breathe underwater?
Could we run really fast?
In this digital land
The fun will always last

Could we have a forever life
And only reset
Or morph from an avatar straight into a pet?
This land would be strange
But could come true
I'd like to explore this land
Wouldn't you?

Amy Jane Clewes (13)

Dreams And Reality

A while ago I dreamed of growing up
Dreamed of fantasy and speculations of how everything would be like
Dreamed of rainbows and clouds made out of magic dust
Glowing skies, blooming sun over my head
Fresh warm air brushing my hair widely
Lush green grass beneath my feet
Vivid flowers swinging in the breeze
I open my eyes, sky stormy dark
Heavy clouds, pouring rain
Dry earth, muddy with sky's tears
Dried leaves, thirsty flowers
I have dreamed for too long, not moved in years
Ivy growing over my bare feet
Frozen gusts of wind try to knock me out
By the cliff, staring at the unending
Chills go down my spine
I close my eyes once more
I only see daylight
I am back.

Lindomar Junio (18)

Imagine If They Knew The Real You...

Imagine if they knew the real you...
The hidden face behind the mask
The sadness behind that smile
The pain you're feeling inside
The constant battle you're fighting within yourself
How you put on a fake smile and answer, "I'm fine!" when you know you're not
How you shut yourself from the world
How you cry yourself to sleep at night
The deep thoughts that play on your mind
The non-stop feeling of exhaustion
The endless feeling of hopelessness
The whispers from the voice inside your head telling you you are not good enough
Just imagine their reaction if they knew the real you.

Beatrice M Opoku (14)

Imagine

Imagine a world, so deep and so dark,
With nothing to do,
But look at the stars.
Imagine, that person might be you that suffers,
You might get all worried.
But that is when, round the corner
A new life awaits.
Imagine if you find this new life,
You must decide one thing...
Good life or bad life?
Only you can decide.
Imagine that it's a good life,
And you become full of joy,
You run to your house,
To start this life.
Oh, one thing to remember...
For when one starts a new life
One must begin a new hobby.
Say that it is painting,
And it works for you,
You can hear Bob Ross' calm, relaxing voice,
For at least thirty minutes of pure peace.

Jensen Warren (11)

Sin Has Come To Play

Imagine if everybody saw each other for what they really are...
Perceptions becoming distortions.
Nightmares becoming reality

Every facade we put on, every mask we wear
Unhinged and distorted beyond our control,
The curtains of friendship, loyalty and truth
Would close on us, the show is done.

Civilisation crumbles to dust
Not so advanced, don't you think?
The past is re-written, the words on a script
The actors come out. The stage is set,
Sin has come to play.

All our demons easing themselves out of the cracks of our souls,
And ready to display themselves to the world,
Human nature is finally revealed
Flaws no longer stories untold.

Carmen Lucia Sánchez Diamente (13)

The Human Condition

The human, faceless automatons haunting endless streets:
Click and whirr.
Stutter and stop.
Muffled to a baseless every day, a bored silence echoing metal emotion.
But imagine
Colour and dreams shot through the choked dark,
bloom prosperous and powerful,
erupt as great as volcanoes, as kind as flowers.
A blossom of creation sparking a beautiful fire; burning humble as the wind.
It drifts to inspire from person to person, friend to friend.
Reaching out to the night, as the sun to the moon.
As if to shake its hearty hand
Chant, loud and free of the light blazing inside people,
Life turned from silence to song.

Amelia Turner (15)

Imagine If...

Imagine if kids oversaw the world,
The rules and laws would change,
The dads would have to be the slaves,
And the mums would be the maids.

Imagine a world without school,
The weekend shall be incessant,
No teachers to boss you around,
And report cards will be never.

Imagine a world without pollution,
And no plastic in the sea,
No wildfires and no terrorists,
What a sublime world it would be.

Presume if you had one desire,
A billion options in your head,
To be rich and to be famous,
Your mind will be tied up like thread.

Imagine that you were a superhero,
What power would you have?
Flying, speed,
The decision is in your hands.

Kevin Galatanu (11)

The Time In-Between

You wait.

It's like you're underwater.
Light bends and blends in a haze,
Sound is muffled,
And words sound stretched and alien.

You wait.

People rush by -
A distorted blur of limbs and faces.
You gaze numbly on,
From behind a thick glass screen.

You wait.

The second-hand hiccups and stutters,
The minute hand drags its feet,
And the hour hand lies inert, not moving,
Except to twitch once in a while.

You wait.

Days are hung with string and just…
Float.
Weeks sway slightly in the wind.
Months are suspended and still.

How long has it been?
Days, weeks, months. Maybe years.
You've forgotten.

You wait.

Connie Harris (15)

Imagine The World Without...

Imagine the world without a sky
To cover humanity as an umbrella
Imagine the world without stars
To decorate the dark sky at night
Imagine the world without the moon
To be our night light
Imagine the world without a sun
To enlighten each of our days
Imagine the world without rain
To help our world to grow
Imagine the world without oxygen
To keep us alive
Imagine the world without trees
To filter the fresh air that we breathe
Imagine the world without pure water
For the wellbeing of everyone
Imagine an empty world
Stop and look
look at the beauty around you
Save our planet for future generations
And let Earth smile again.

Mouna-Myriam Coulibaly (12)

Fog Grey Utopia

We hear a foreign breeze
Lacerate my absent,
Antique feel of ease.

Lachrymal essence
We hear, that can't abide to cease
The trickles of their dolent beads.

We don't but hear, blunt creases
In our ponders; with our dolour, yonder it leads
Astray with social reticence.

If all were sown with happy seeds,
Creditted for our every contrivance,
Declared an equipoise for reigned and reeds
To treat rights and wrongs to peace-

This veil we've worn for centuries,
Never known from whence it's forged...
May you, or not, or nigh; to bidding us, our last goodbye.

Kewen Wang (17)

Just Imagine

Have you ever laid in bed,
Your pillow resting under your head,
Just imagining what the world could be,
In our society,
People are judged by their colour,
Everyone has to be ashamed of their gender,
Girl are insecure while boys are on top,
Or it is switched,
We have to stop,
You can't judge someone by their looks,
When you're not in the book,
Girls are hurt every day,
Boys are the same,
Imagine how you would feel,
If these weren't real,
Nothing can control us,
When we are not meant to be controlled,
You make your story,
By believing in yourself,
So who are you?
That is what life is all about.

Mairghréad Hodgkinson-Bostock (11)

Boredom

I go off to my own worlds when I am bored.
Where I battle dragons with a shield and sword!
Or become a queen, ruling the land
Maybe on holiday running in sand.

On a night, I go to the past;
Meet Curie and Antoinette (that goes by fast)
Shakespeare talks about his plays;
The six wives I could listen to for days.

When I'm in school I become a millionaire.
I love when I am an actress - so fair.
I control what I am sometimes;
That's when I'm a poet, using awesome rhymes

Imagination is the key,
There are so many ways to set it free;
Like: songs, books or poetry.
So be as creative as you can be.

Isobelle Hartley (12)

Imagine A World Ruled By Love...

Imagine those who you loved,
also truly loved you.
The world would be so blessed
for everyone around you.

Let's be good to each other,
we aren't guaranteed tomorrow,
so when we have left the world
we would be gone with no sorrow.

Imagine the happy moments,
captured with your camera lens,
when you look back at them
they give your soul a good cleanse.

Being known for your kindness
is a blessing on its own.
Why don't you show it often
and proudly wear it like a crown?

Imagine if in our world
love was given unconditionally,
then we wouldn't worry about
being ourselves casually!

Helen Mohammed (18)

Imagine A World

Imagine a world; a stress-free world,
A world with no deadly viruses or worries.
A world where freedom can be guaranteed to anyone.

Imagine a world where masks weren't
An everyday essential item,
A world where we could freely meet our friends and family.

Imagine a world where we wouldn't sit before our TVs listening to the
Amount of deaths, and cases, and the need for help,
While being locked up with our own problems.

Imagine a world where finally inner peace will surround us,
And we could finally share the Christmas spirit
With our loved ones.

I believe imagination has no limits.

Tiffani Eluka (13)

Imagine

What if animals could talk?
Imagine what they would say!
Would they tell us how they feel
Or would they tell us about their day?

Would they tell us if they're happy?
Would they tell us if they're sad?
Would they tell us if they're angry
Or tell us when they're glad?

If they were feeling silly
Would they get up and dance?
Would they get on an aeroplane
And fly all the way to France?

However they would feel
I would just have to say
This would be total chaos
Even just for one day.

Emily Clewes (11)

Betrayal

Betrayal, deception, treachery
I gave all that I had trusting your very soul
But you turned your back
And whispered every word
You ruined it all you cold-hearted fool
And threw me to the lions with a grimace
It bit and slew me with poison
Into every flesh, every bone
I cried in misery and agony hoping you would come
But you never did
I have not any words to say
But beware, my friend, I will walk with rage
Making you beg for mercy
I imagine making you my only prey
Making you suffer like I did
And I will relish every one of your hideous howls
This is only my warning...

Puhalovian Tharshan (11)

Just Imagine...

Imagine,
You could time travel,
You could go back in time,
You could experience a different era,
You could see a different point of view,

Imagine,
Dreams could become true,
Dreams would be a reality,
Dreams filled with chocolate rivers,
Dreams filled with princesses and castles,

Imagine,
Humans were extinct,
Animals would have their own language,
Animals would rule the world,
Animals would remould the world,

Imagine,
You were immortal,
You would live forever,
You would get to see the world develop,
You would experience great change,

Imagine, just imagine...

Amna Ramzan (13)

If I Ruled The World

If I ruled the world,
It would be a different place
Homework would be banned for evermore,
Electric cars around the world
Pollution would stop
So we could be safe and stay alive
COVID would be gone
Demolished by the vaccine
So everyone could do what they loved again
Robots would take care of your house,
So you could sit back and relax
Uniforms would be in the past
All clothes would be back
All turtles can do now is choke on plastic,
If I ruled the world
No more of it would be in existence
If I could rule the world,
It would be a different place.

Eshal Raza (12)

If I Were Invisible

If I were invisible
I would go around the world
Without anyone knowing
I would play pranks on people
So that I would be annoying
I could help people
Like giving them food and money to make them happy
Also not forgetting that one boy called Jakey!
Being invisible wouldn't be so bad
Then again you might have to think back
I said to somebody hello but they didn't answer back
I smiled at someone in the hall but they didn't smile back
So that's what it's like being invisible!

Joel Ige (11)

Imagine If You Were Immortal

Millions of years have passed;
How long has it been?
It's been centuries, no, millennia since I last
Touched human skin

I've seen the rise and fall of planets,
And wandered among the stars,
Yet nothing was more poetic,
Than the calm after the destruction of Mars,

I've seen galaxies being born,
All this while feeling forlorn,
I watched them die;
All I did was cry.

I've travelled the universe,
Explored the depths of time and space
Yet, nothing, nothing
Could have granted me peace

It is truly horrible
Imagine if you were immortal

Kishore Satheeskumar (13)

Imagine

Imagine being the youngest with no one to play with,
Imagine sitting there bored each day with nothing to do,
Imagine having a sister to do all those things with you
Imagine...

Imagine having a sibling to do the same things as you.
Playing together and bored never
Having fun each day, every day
Always together, forever.

Imagine how much happier you would be,
Smiling, laughing, never alone
Imagine soaring through the sky
With a sibling by your side

The world would be a better place with me and you
A sibling would change my world
Just imagine...

Sumaiyah Mahmood (12)

The Wonders Of Imagination

Oh, what wonder it is to fantasise
Power to create anything at will
What glee, what wonder
What a wonderful, colourful imagination

Just imagine
Being on a boat long at sea
On a journey to the great blue sea
Seeing fish far and wide
Finding riches beyond wonder

Just imagine
The wild wild west far from sea
Tumbleweed close and far
Gunslinging for honour and fame
Wild and yet still tame

Just imagine
Just imagine, being the boss of your own dream
Being the creator of what you dream
What a wonderful time to imagine
What a wonderful time to dream.

Antonio Ursanu (15)

The Inquisition Of Activism

Admirable freedom, equality and justice.
Our collective fantasy illusion
In no metric is it achievable.
Clamber out from the chest
And hurtle towards reality, with me.
Observe
The poverty,
The privilege handed discriminately,
The necessities needed desperately,
And yet where are we?
Reluctantly transformed into activism
With no partnering action
Honouring the problem
While we're full with dissatisfaction
Desiring something had been done.
In the future, I hope we learn
The only way is proactivity.
No room for reluctancy and dependency.

George Randall

Imagination

I f only one day your dream would come true
M aybe you wish for a special moment or two
A lthough you may seem to give up
G uaranteed you still have hope
I nside you, even the tiniest speck will grant your wish
N ever ever will you fail
A ll the wishes range from big to small
T o not know what your wish is yet is okay
I mpossible they say
O nly you know that an impossibility is a possibility to be explored
N ow you know all about wishes, what is yours?

Ruby Casemore (12)

Imagine Me!

I am artistic
As well as thoughtful
I'm stylish when I want to be
And lazy almost every day

I love BTS
A k-pop boy band
They're amazing music
Helps me to keep my cool

I live with my mum and dad
My awesome superheroes
And my younger sister
Taking my things forever

I don't like school
In fact, I despise it
I only come for my friends
And also lunch and break

My favourite colour is purple
Like lavenders in fields
All my things are purple
Even my hair!

I hope you like my poem
Since it's all about me!

Esha Malik

Imagine If...

Imagine if everyone was equal;
there would be no racism, sexism, religious prosecution, homophobic people, transphobic people.

Imagine if everyone was happy;
there would be no sadness, mental health issues, wars.

Imagine if bullying didn't exist;
there would be no suicide, depression, social anxiety.

Imagine if crime wasn't an issue;
there would be no reason for prisons, there would be no stealing, burglary, murder, heresy, arson.

Imagine if the world was perfect.

Just imagine if...

Ellie-Jayne Scott (12)

History

History has always been set in stone,
But what if we could change that?
The kings and queens overthrown,
Everything we know just gone like that.

The history books would be rewritten,
No one knowing the exact truth,
Everything would seem like fiction,
Nothing would seem real anymore.

The world as we know it,
The culture we've grown up with,
Everything we've ever known,
Just gone like that.

Just imagine what could happen,
If everything turned upside down,
Life as we know it gone like that,
Just imagine.

Katie Riley (14)

Imagine

Imagine that the world ended tomorrow,
But then we would be asking for forgiveness in sorrow,
Imagine that we had anything in the world,
But then our minds would've been twisted and twirled,
Imagine that we had something but wanted more,
But then we would go on a rampage and chomp and roar,
Imagine that we always wanted to win but never wanted to lose,
But then you would find yourself taking insults and boos,

Always imagine and always dream,
But remember, things won't come out as good as they seem...

Mikayeel Malik (13)

The Plague Doctor's Love

Like an inescapable feeling of perpetual death,
his rapier at his heel,
the night dissolves his ghostly breath,
shadows dance in his appeal,
yet in the depths,
his heart could not yet steal,
the girl who was always vexed,
and stubborn to his ideal,

unbowed to fate,
yet bent by loves uncalming hand,
ever-shaken in a blissful state,
his end betrothed to all things bland,
but alas his profession came too late,
his fruitless efforts manned,

and the girl who drank in the tavern,
became nothing more than sand.

Amber Glease (13)

A World I'm Known For!

I close my eyes and then I see
a word so beautiful, just you and me.
The sun is bright and the colours are clear
I know my dear you are near.
I start running and I find a treat.
A lollipop is it or ice cream?
I look away and see a star
I know the dark is close enough.
A fairy comes towards me.
She asks me what my dream life will be
I tell her that I'm very pleased
she smiles
a bit later I wake up and see my pet
and know we are back home.

Anestina Alexiadou

Ode To Each Utopia

Daemons bind to each their own Utopia.
Faustian vanity clots like blood in their brutish forms,
Yet shivering in glory of claret sin.
Liminal - flaking gold rust - the scales of misadventure.
The wager shifts, unfulfilled and petulant, between the waking hours.
And bickers between each earlobe: Latin and jargon and foul lies.
Stooped in green hedonism, the soft centre of antiquity.
Pacts wedged amongst consonants, slacks and nosedives of Soul-like penance.
What a sorry state of promise we embody!

Madeleine Wren Friedlein (16)

Imagine A World Full Of Conflict And War

Imagine a world full of conflict and war,
Gunshots and blood everywhere,
Some soldiers are found so near Death's door,
And the sirens just fill up the air.

The spirit has gone down to zero percent,
And the children are crying in fear,
The soldiers are all trying to shake off the scent,
For their enemies are really quite near.

The ruins of houses fill up the street,
The bombs have destroyed them all,
All the soldiers are thinking revenge is quite sweet,
But in reality it's exceedingly cruel.

Lydia Wilkins (12)

Imagine

Imagine you had one wish,
Well what would it be,
"I wish I had a pet fish!"
Actually, make that three!

Imagine you had one wish,
I'd wish I had lots of money,
I'd hire a chef to cook me a dish,
He'd make it out of tunny.

Imagine you had one wish,
I'd wish my family could be famous,
Something, we'd accomplish,
Never again will we be called ignoramus.

Imagine you had one wish,
What is It, that's the question?
Nothing too outlandish,
Have a little discretion.

Manraj Tagar (11)

If Dreams Were Real

If dreams were real
And if they came true
I would live in my own little world filled with exciting things
It's a world with music
That flows through my ears
In my world there's lots of cake and video games
I can fly anywhere and go to my favourite places
It's a place I can have fun and enjoy myself
But even though this place isn't real
And it's only my imagination
I would visit there again
And again in my dreams!

Daniel Ige (13)

Listening

Listening
Thinking about a poem that might change something
But I wasn't thinking about listening
To the world that was talking
To the wildlife that was singing
To the nature that was suffering
To the people that were dying
To the animals that were crying
So I started listening
And hearing
But were any of us listening?
We were all
Fighting
Shouting
Screaming
Arguing
We have a lot of problems
But we will have solutions
If we start
Listening
We might start
Hearing.

Salman Hussein (13)

If... You Could Teleport

I would travel from country to country
and win every single race.
Even though this might be cheating,
I will still be the same at eating.
I would travel to Mars and visit a couple of bars.
I wouldn't be late for school
and everybody would think I was cool.
I could teleport to a pool
or go to a shop and get a free tool.
I bet you are thinking: *this is an impossible pace!*
But just imagine if this were the case!
All you have to do is imagine, just imagine...

Timothy Robb (11)

Imagine If The Sun Burns Out

Befriend the light while it shines on your face,
And the heat, even if on your back it leaves a painful trace,
The flowers in their seasonal bloom,
Without the sun our fate is doom.

Because if the sun burns out,
Everyone will die throughout,
The world will drop colder than you think you know,
And there will be no tomorrow.

So enjoy your summers on the boiling hot beaches,
And your fruit salads with the ripest of peaches,
But always beware,
Of life without the sun's glare.

Poppy Taylor (11)

Flower Buds Are Trampled

Slipping and sliding in the mud,
Flower buds are trampled,
Soldiers crossing borders with guns firing as loud as their orders,
The unknown enemy awaits
With plans to stop their opposition's food and freight,
But they will pay for those who created this fraud,
Will never live to go back home abroad,
Another day done as the sun sets,
On the blood of many men from either side,
At home women and children weep
Over those who have gone to forever sleep
And will never come home.

Calum McLennan

What If Children Ruled The World?

What if children ruled the world?
What do you think would unfurl?
What would they eat?
Would their diet consist of sweets?
Where would they live?
How much would they give?
Never mind, new growth
Don't do what they are told
What fun, what joy
Forever new toys
Innocence, truth
Out with the old, in with the new
Doesn't matter who or why
Only looking at the bright side
What if children ruled the world?

Lucy Seaman (13)

Imagine

Imagine there was no Heaven,
Life would be so easy,
There would be no Hell,
People would never have to worry again.

Imagine there were no countries,
Everybody would live in the same place,
There would be no war,
Everybody would be equal.

Imagine there was no life,
The world would be so quiet,
So dull,
And lifeless.

Imagine that everyone was rich,
There would be no thieves,
No homeless people,
No people left hungry on the cold, lonely streets,
Everyone would be the same.

Rahil Shabibiul (11)

Imagine

Imagine we could travel inside books
Then I'll be dancing with Belle and the Beast
Who judge none by their looks
I'll be working with Cinderella preparing a feast
Who is more cheerful than all the cooks
I'll be casting spells with Elsa and Tink
And Beauty would clap without sleeping a wink
Battle the witches, I'll try my best
Evil plans of the north and west
Prince Charming and I will reveal all their links
Just imagine we could travel inside books!

Mengtong Yin (13)

Imagining Just Cheese

Oh I, oh I, oh I, oh I,
I am in love with your taste,
Oh I, oh I, oh I, oh I,
I am in love with your taste.
Just cheese
Spicy, salty, nutty, creamy, fruity cheese,
I am in love with your smell,
In addition to the shape of you,
Especially Yorkshire Blue.
Just cheese,
Grated, sliced, cubed, stringy, melted,
I'm not bothered,
Crusty cheese, cheese sandwich, cheese pizza,
I can eat them all day long.
Just imagine how long I could survive without my gorgeous cheese.

Ethan Ramful (11)

Imagine...

- **I** magine yourself floating around in outer space.
- **M** aybe you're above an unexplored planet,
- **A** steroids whizzing past planets at break-neck speed,
- **G** aining momentum as you fall through the dense layer of toxic gases,
- **I** nstantly the reeks of the gases knock you out unconscious,
- **N** othing can be heard, felt or seen,
- **E** ventually you wake up back on Earth, engulfed by a mob of people shocked by what they are witnessing.

Manjot Kaur (14)

Imagine A World..

Imagine a world without hate,
The world would be such a better place,
Imagine a world with a clean sea.
Just clean water and no waste,
Imagine a world with peace,
Where everyone learned to love.
Imagine a world with happiness.
Even from those above.
Imagine a world without litter,
Where everyone learned to use a bin.
Imagine a world without racism,
Where people weren't judged by the colour of their skin.

Christian-Michael Frimpong-Mainoo (12)

The Curse Of An Immortal Blessing

A man once overcame death,
a lengthy time ago.
He thought leisure was his
but immortality has great sorrow.

It started off with jubilance,
with Time as a friend.
All knowledge at his grasp
but what's the point of life with no end?

The families he's had,
the memories born,
Time is no friend,
but a killer with no remorse.

His eyes, tinted with regret
His smile gone dull,
Here is a statue, no man.
Immortality is a curse afterall...

Zane Attwal (14)

Imagine

Imagine!

Imagine if there was no life on Earth
imagine if we never existed,
Imagine if we never had power,
Imagine that!

But that's not real, that's not true
Because we do exist and we do have power
- a lot of it
Imagine that!

Ninety-two million cars are being produced worldwide,
- the ecosystem is collapsing while our greed is growing
Imagine that!

We need to act now
let's not imagine that...

Ameille Hayoukane (12)

World Cup Winner

W hat if I scored a goal
O n the grandest stage of them all?
R ight in the top corner
L uck is on my side
D oing what I do best

C lapping all around me
U p and down
P eople lifting me up

W e've won, we've won
I n celebration we praise each other
N ow we're here
N ow it's clear
E veryone side by side
R ight where we belong.

Sam Stokes (11)

Just Imagine

I go into my favourite roller coaster
My mind projects videos.
And sucks me into them:
Goal! One point to us (the aliens)
Let's go!
I'm flying like Superman.
No school forever!
Amazing! Toilet detergent is edible!
The tale of Mulan starred by me!
I hear a stern voice:
"Oh Jayden, stop daydreaming!"
"No, I'm not daydreaming, Miss Yayle.
I am working on my 'Imagine' poem."

Jeremiel Mbogol (11)

Just Imagine Being Free

Imagine watching your thoughts come to life whenever
Imagine shaking hands with the hero of your dreams
Imagine never having to say never
Imagine everyone as one big team

Imagine the future
Imagine it becomes your present
Imagine preventing all torture
Imagine erasing the word peasant

Imagine being free
Imagine being relaxed
Imagine swimming in the tropical sea
Imagine not having to be scared

Just imagine being free.

Paulo Alexys Gonçalves (12)

Flying Over The Stars...

I wonder
If I could reach the stars
If I just stretched high enough
I could maybe imagine
That I was touching the stars
I wonder
Why the galaxy is endless
If I imagined hard enough
I could see
A mini-me
On a parallel Earth
In a parallel universe
Why if I imagined hard enough I could see
An alien waving to me
From a far-off planet
And if I imagined just a tiny bit more
I could see myself
Soaring over the stars.

Hawwaa Bint Mahmood (17)

Imagine

Imagine a world of your creation,
A reality that can be whatever you like,
A landscape filled with joys and wonders,
Filled with pure delight.

Imagine a landscape dead with decay,
With bones and broken promises,
A single lost soul amongst the murder,
Trapped in a solitary solstice.

Imagine those worlds colliding,
Happiness meeting sorrow,
Hope meeting misery,
All run through with a single clear arrow.

Poppy Cooper (13)

Wonderland Of Words

I sit and read
The many books
That I have read before
No matter how much I read them
I can still read them once more.

The plump red chair surrounds me
As I dream about my fairy tale
That wonderful magical day
When my mind grew wings and flew away.

An old lady walks past
As she draws me back to reality
She said the library is going to close now
But you can borrow a book
To be in your little fantasy.

Suzie Jones (11)

Under The Sea

I glide through the sea
The cool water swirling around me
In a colourful world no one can see
It's another world under here
The water so blue and clear
Other fishes swimming near
The sun glinting on their scales
Dots of colour on their tails
Under the sea it's bright with colour
I wish I could stay here forever
I need to come back to reality
But I know I can return back to the sea.

Asma Siddika

I Wish

Imagine you had one wish,
What would it be?

What about a genie,
Sitting at the back,
With his head down,
Looking like a clown.

Imagine your name is Will,
But where is Big Jill?

Imagine granting wishes,
Just stick to the dishes.

Imagine looking like a beast,
Just because you live in the east.

Imagine you are peacefully sleeping,
Your teacher screeching, "Stop peeping!"

Reece Roper

Imagine Ultraman - The Avatar

U nstoppable, ultimate avatar of the crown
L oving superhero in the town
T errific man is always there for everyone
R avishing champion who is unknown
A mazing is the other name he owns
M arvellous warrior in the Justice League zone
A dventurous fights he has using his drones
N on-defeatable hero who has ever been born!

Izaan Ahamed (12)

War Brings Endings

Imagine you were groaning in agony
Imagine you'd die in vanity
Imagine a dagger protruding your chest
Imagine you tried to be the very best

Imagine soldiers running to your aid
Imagine them screaming, "General, please don't fade."
Imagine if you knew your faith
Imagine you were under a stone with a wraith.

Affan Aflar (12)

Imagine If Dreams Didn't Come True

Imagine if dreams didn't come true,
Wendy wouldn't have flew,
Cinderella wouldn't have met her Prince Charming,
Snow White's stepmother would be non-harming,
Jack wouldn't have climbed up the beanstalk,
The tortoise wouldn't have won the race because of how slow he could walk,
How dreadful would it be if these dreams didn't come true.

Summer Houston-Earl

Those Eyes

The flames in them burn,
the rain in them loves,
they shine in the sun
and they hurt in the snow.

They close to erase
the memory I hold
of those pained days
when I felt I was lost.

I had to be different
I had to be strong
I closed my eyes then
and I knew I needed more.

Those eyes that hate
those eyes that love
those eyes can lie
but can show you the world.

Chrysa Tsantikou (15)

If I Was A Teacher...

If I was a teacher,
That would be weird,
I hated being a student,
But this is what I feared!

If I was a teacher,
Wake up at six,
Grab a coffee on the go,
Get my caffeine fix.

If I was a teacher,
Drive in the awful weather,
Shout at rowdy kids,
I'm at the end of my tether.

If I was a teacher,
Come home at seven,
Marked a few books,
Now it's eleven!

Layla Rashid (12)

Dream On...

Imagine,
Imagine what the world would be like without mankind,
No inventions,
No fire,
No discoveries,

Imagine,
Imagine what the world would be like if dreams were real,
Life would be crazy,
Everyone would go crazy,
And you would go crazy,

Imagine,
Imagine if you could change history,
You could change the world for good or bad,
But you have the choice.

Muhammad Haroon Ramzan (11)

Dreams

I magine if you had invisibility
M aybe you could have all the ice cream in the world
A professional cake baker
G etting to have a shopping centre in the basement
I f you could be a billionaire
N ever having to go to bed, no rules
E verybody could be full of surprises.

Ramlah Ahsan (11)

Attack Of The Titans

I magine if they knew the real me
M y hands are full of my own blood
A gain, more Titans to attack
G reat, I'm running low on energy
I magine if my friends experienced pain like this
N o! Another fight is occurring
E xcellent work team! I think they're gone!

Amy Lee Smith (12)

Imagine Being Immortal

Imagine being alone,
Imagine waking up to the same thing every day,
Feeling like nothing could hurt you now,
Dreading a sign,
Seeking hope,
Living in a reality which seems so fictitious,
But now feels murderous,
Reminiscing unforgettable memories,
Having no sense of identity,
Who am I?
Who was I?
Who will I be?

Mehak Khalique (14)

If I Were A Wolf

I 'd run around all day
F inding my prey

I have some friends

W e eat our food
E at all day
R ay of sun
E ager to hunt

A re particularly good players

W olves are fluffy
O n the run
L ong sense of smell
F ast legs.

Keely Rodda (13)

The Worry Wave

Worry is a wave
Constantly lapping at my toes
A forsaken mutt
Reeking of smothering silence
Sometimes it catches me off guard
Then... *whoosh!*
Paralysed, contorted
And I'm left coughing, spluttering, gasping
So wave goodbye.
Until we smile again my friend...

Jessica Ilott (14)

The Power Of Invisibility

To be invisible
And without a care,
Can be a struggle
And lead to despair.

To be unseen
And overlooked,
Can be great at fourteen
But you can get hooked.

To be disguised
And wear a mask,
You would be surprised
At the perilous task.

To be invisible - it's pivotal.

Sneha Godhaniya (14)

What Would You Buy With A Million Pounds?

What would you buy with a million pounds?
A car?
A mat?
Or maybe a house?
Let's try something more elaborate.
A dog?
A cat?
A tiny mouse?
Whatever you buy, just hold it quite true,
That all this money is not only for you.

Samanta Gerulskyte (18)

Imagining Rumsby-Ferris

When we did walk,
I loved to talk,
But when we finished,
I could not flee,
As I stared at what was beyond the given tree,
A precious girl,
I could not tell,
How I felt,
When suddenly, my heart did melt.

Ashley Smith (16)

YOUNG WRITERS INFORMATION

We hope you have enjoyed reading this book – and that you will continue to in the coming years.

If you're a young writer who enjoys reading and creative writing, or the parent of an enthusiastic poet or story writer, do visit our website **www.youngwriters.co.uk**. Here you will find free competitions, workshops and games, as well as recommended reads, a poetry glossary and our blog. There's lots to keep budding writers motivated to write!

If you would like to order further copies of this book, or any of our other titles, then please give us a call or order via your online account.

Young Writers
Remus House
Coltsfoot Drive
Peterborough
PE2 9BF
(01733) 890066
info@youngwriters.co.uk

Join in the conversation!
Tips, news, giveaways and much more!

YoungWritersUK   @YoungWritersCW   @YoungWritersCW